DK Annotated Guides

ARCHITECTURE

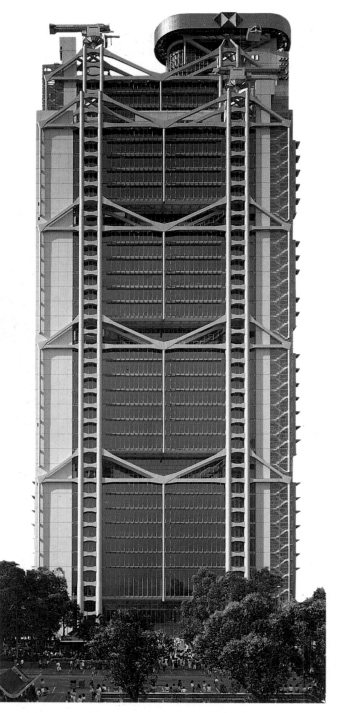

Hong Kong and Shanghai Bank
See page 100

ARCHITECTURE

NEIL STEVENSON

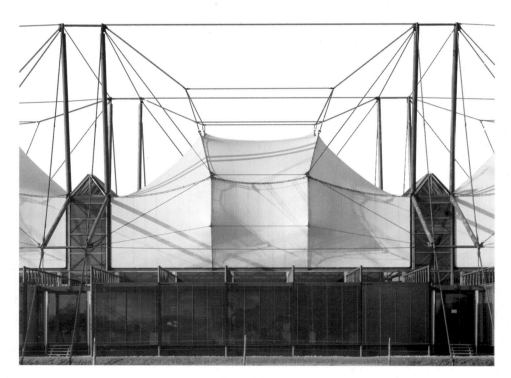

Detail from
*Schlumberger Cambridge
Research Centre*
See page 102

Detail from
Durham Cathedral
See page 26

DK PUBLISHING, INC.

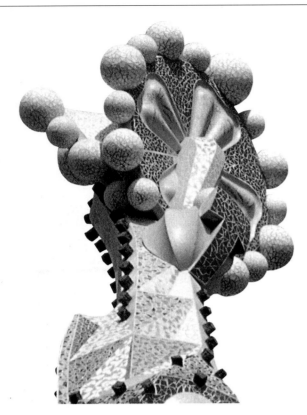

A DK PUBLISHING BOOK

Art Editor Simon Murrell
Project Editor Neil Lockley
Editor Julie Oughton
US Editor Irene Pavitt
Managing Editors Gwen Edmonds,
Christine Winters
Senior Managing Editor Sean Moore
Deputy Art Director Tina Vaughan
Production Controller Sarah Coltman
Picture Researcher Deborah Pownall

Detail from
Sagrada Familia
See page 72

Detail from
The Alhambra
See page 34

Detail from
Castle Howard
See page 60

First American Edition, 1997
2 4 6 8 10 9 7 5 3
Published in the United States by
DK Publishing Inc., 95 Madison Avenue,
New York, New York 10016

Visit us on the World Wide Web at
http://www.dk.com

Copyright © 1997
Dorling Kindersley Limited, London

Library of Congress
Cataloging-in-Publication Data

Stevenson, Neil.
Architecture / by Neil Stevenson.
p.   cm. — (Annotated guides)
Includes index.
ISBN 0-7894-1965-3
1. Architecture—History.   I. Title.   II. Series.
NA200.S72   1997
720—dc21   97-16174

Reproduced by GRB Editrice s.r.l.
Printed in Italy by A. Mondadori, Verona

Detail from
Krak des Chevaliers
See page 30

Detail from
The Pompidou Center
See page 96

CONTENTS

Looking at Architecture **6**

Temple of Amun,
Karnak **8**

The Parthenon **10**

The Colosseum **12**

The Pantheon **14**

Ise Shrine **16**

Santa Sophia **18**

Temple I, Tikal **20**

Kandariya Mahadev
Temple, Khajuraho **22**

Pisa Cathedral **24**

Durham Cathedral **26**

Angkor Wat **28**

Krak des Chevaliers **30**

Notre-Dame,
Paris **32**

The Alhambra **34**

Florence Cathedral **36**

Temple of Heaven **38**

King's College
Chapel **40**

Tempietto
San Pietro **42**

St. Peter's, Rome **44**

St. Basil's
Cathedral **46**

Villa Rotonda **48**

Hardwick Hall **50**

Katsura Palace **52**

The Taj Mahal **54**

Potala Palace **56**

St. Paul's Cathedral **58**

Castle Howard **60**

Royal Pavilion **62**

Altes Museum **64**

The Houses
of Parliament **66**

Crystal Palace **68**

Turbine Building,
Menier Factory **70**

Sagrada Familia **72**

Glasgow School
of Art **74**

Gamble House **76**

Robie House **78**

Castle Drogo **80**

Schröder House **82**

Villa Savoye **84**

Empire State
Building **86**

Villa Mairea **88**

Farnsworth House **90**

Sydney Opera House **92**

Tokyo Olympic Stadium **94**

The Pompidou Center **96**

Neue Staatsgalerie **98**

Hong Kong and
Shanghai Bank **100**

Schlumberger Cambridge
Research Centre **102**

The Ark **104**

Kansai International
Airport Terminal **106**

Glossary **108**

Index **110**

Acknowledgments **112**

Detail from
Hong Kong and Shanghai Bank
See page 100

Detail from
King's College Chapel
See page 40

Detail from
Neue Staatsgalerie
See page 98

LOOKING AT ARCHITECTURE

The constant stream of images that pass to us from films, television, books, and magazines allows us superficial acquaintance with many of the world's great architectural landmarks. Possibilities for international travel – expanded through pilgrimage, trade, and tourism – have brought many of these buildings within reach of a wider audience. The buildings that surround us in our daily lives earn a familiarity of a different kind, however. In both instances, the opportunity to pause and look again, supplemented by some additional information, can be greatly rewarding to our curiosity and general understanding. Making sense of architecture requires some capacity for objective assessment – to stand back from the building and consider aspects of its physical presence.

The Parthenon (447–432 BC)
Classical Greek and Roman precedents have exerted a continual influence on Western architecture. The Parthenon summarizes the aesthetic refinements of Classical Greece.

Familiarity Throughout this book, consideration is given to form, general organization, materials and methods of construction, principles of structure, and stylistic and decorative features. But few buildings are examples merely of inhabited sculpture, and the *function* and *context* of a building are of fundamental purpose and importance in their appreciation. For this reason, buildings are more easily understood when we see them in use and consider them *in situ*.

Architecture is handed down to us in a "used" condition and is subject to a continual process of evolution. While this may obscure the original work, this process is equally revealing of the developments and cultural preferences of successive generations. On close inspection, buildings can often reveal the results of modification and rebuilding.

To make some sense of the bewildering profusion of historical styles, any study of architecture necessarily has a starting position and a particular sense of direction. The story of Western architecture emerged from the reconstructed fragments of ancient Egypt, Classical Greece, and the Roman Empire; Western perspectives have traditionally inclined toward Classical architecture and the Greco-Roman model. Until the 19th century, Gothic architecture was often considered to be the product of a dark and uncivilized age. The 19th-century revival of academic interest in the medieval world produced a categorization of the development of the European Gothic, including a recognition of Byzantine and Romanesque traditions. Modern architecture, developing in the early 20th century from impulses resulting from the Industrial Revolution, polarized attitudes into nostalgic and antihistoric tendencies. While the first idealized Romantic pasts, the second plotted new beginnings on sheets of white paper. Postmodern culture is more pluralistic, however, permitting simultaneously a number of different viewpoints, even when they are taken from the same cultural starting position.

Tempietto San Pietro (1502–10)
Renaissance architecture expanded the Classical architectural vocabulary, seeking a new expression through mathematical order and harmonic proportion.

Surviving Evidence Our interpretation of architectural history is prejudiced by surviving evidence. The priority given to monumental, masonry architecture is, in part, due to the imperishable nature of its construction. Increasingly sophisticated methods of archaeological analysis are giving new insights into other cultures, which use, or have used timber, fabric, mud, and whatever else to construct their built environments. History, particularly architectural history, is made possible by surviving artifacts – and the material remnants of a society, even when their significance is lost, help to fire our imagination.

Ways of Seeing In the 17th century, the English traveler, scholar, and poet Sir Henry Wotton (1568–1639) defined architecture as having the prerequisite conditions of "firmness, commodity and delight." "Firmness" here is the method of support and construction; "commodity," the suitability of the design to the purpose; and "delight," the emotional response to its execution. This definition has held up remarkably well, although shifting ground slightly to accompany the pace of Western industrial society.

In the late 19th century, the American architect Louis Sullivan (1856–1924) made the observation that "form follows function," reflecting the search for efficient methods of delivering the new building types required by a rapidly industrialized society. In the 20th century, Le Corbusier (1887–1966) defined architecture as the "masterly, correct, and magnificent play of masses brought together in light", elevating architectural form to a spiritual plane. But society has not always regarded new ideas with such urgency. For example, the slow evolution of ancient Egyptian architecture was related to a spiritual constancy that developed, and then enshrined, particular architectural types that prevailed for many centuries. Our modern-day perspective is much more immediate. We can see, therefore, that the analysis of construction, function, and form is helpful in tracing architectural development through successive periods. The examples in this book give consideration to these aspects, as they form recognizable characteristics of appearance and provide a means of classification.

While the scrutiny of technology is fascinating and revealing, it disposes a characteristically modern view. The spiritual value of many historic buildings was often of much greater significance to their original constructors than was the means of building them. While technical accounts of ancient building methods are not unknown, architectural prestige rests more with the commissioning client and the commemorative aspects of the building than with the names or methods of its constructors. The cults of individuals, personal styles, and schools of architecture became more apparent with the rise in status of the artist during the Renaissance, when methods of architecture began to change. Conventional drawings in plan, elevation, and section, accompanied by detailed models, began to conceptualize the building as a unified work, feasibly undertaken for a single client and supervised by a single architect. St. Paul's Cathedral (see p. 58) in London was the first major cathedral to be built under such a regime, at the height of the English Renaissance. As construction programs become increasingly urgent and complex, the method and quantification of such projects become more intrusive and influential in the manifestation of the architecture. Ancient practices, which relied on large numbers of people using simple technology, have given way to modern methods involving fewer people with a reliance on sophisticated methods and unique solutions.

The issues of appropriate technology and self-sustainability have a determining influence on the way buildings look and perform. The phenomenal amount of energy invested in the origination and servicing of buildings has come under close scrutiny. Environmental issues are certain to dominate architectural debate for some time, as are the techniques of designing in a computer-literate world. This reorientation may prove to be a redeeming factor, helping to overcome some of the conservative tendencies prevalent in some societies wishing to preserve everything, irrespective of merit. Elsewhere, it may engender a more appropriate response to climate and culture, working in recognition of context and environment. The imbalance of either condition threatens to blight our contemporary contribution to architectural heritage.

Recurrent Themes

Certain subjects emerge as being particularly instructive to the periodic developments in architecture. The dome, for example, occurs frequently in the architectural vocabulary of many civilizations. It possesses a natural,

The Chrysler Building (1928–30)
The skyscrapers of the 1930s were an enduring contribution to monumental architecture. Our modern regard for creativity and technological progress is mirrored in the developments of architecture during the past few decades.

Kansai International Airport Terminal (1991–94)
This conceptually simple design resolves a complex problem. The scale and pace of development illustrate the capacity for architecture to challenge human ingenuity and its faculty for cooperative effort.

elemental geometry, derived from the most compact unit of enclosure, the sphere. It occurs frequently throughout the sacred architecture of ancient and modern cultures and has been attributed religious, humanistic, and natural properties.

The individual dwelling house has been endlessly interpreted by architects throughout history. The flexibility of the form provided architects with opportunities for experiment and investigation, generating ideas that may later emerge as seminal influences on subsequent trends. Religious buildings have a special place in architectural history too. In Western architecture, the evolution of the Christian church, from the earliest meeting halls to the splendor of the Baroque, provides a fascinating account of human achievement. A similar account can be found in the architecture of the many other religions, from the delicate geometry of the Islamic mosque to the contemplative beauty of the Buddhist temple.

The significance of architecture is not, of course, restricted to a limited number of distinguished buildings. A curiosity in the buildings that surround us will reveal an inevitable measure of delight. The most significant aspect of looking at buildings is in what we glean about the societies that built them. Their technologies and methods of social organization, their practical needs and idealistic desires – all are recorded in the fabric of their buildings. Both the course of architectural history and the state of architecture today reveal the irrepressible nature of human ingenuity and humanity's faculty for collaborative effort.

TEMPLE OF AMUN, KARNAK

ALTHOUGH WITH ONLY PRIMITIVE TOOLS and an army of enslaved laborers, the ancient Egyptians were among the most prolific builders in history. Through the erection of monumental projects, such as temples, they followed a profound religious conviction to honor and appease their gods. Temples dedicated to the gods and ancestral worship were often constructed in stages, periodically remodeled to accommodate grander schemes. At the Temple of Amun, Karnak, Egypt (1530–323 BC), the buildings are arranged along processional routes connected to the Nile quayside and the nearby temple site of Luxor. The sanctuary is approached through a succession of open courts and the hypostyle hall. The central avenue of the hall had clerestory lighting, with the surrounding columns receding into the vast, dark interior. The inner sanctuary housed the sacred effigy of the creator god, Amun, attended by the pharaoh and the priesthood with their secretive rites. The 53-acre (21.4-hectare) precinct was erected over a period of 1,200 years, monumentally recording the pharaoh's dynastic struggle for immortality.

Decoration
The columns and surfaces throughout the hypostyle hall were carved with richly colored and incised relief designs illustrating dynastic triumphs, scenes from ceremonies, and daily life. Images, statues, and sculpted panels were habitually defaced, and identifying hieroglyphics were usurped by succeeding pharaohs seeking to reinforce their own lineage and personality cult.

PYLONS
The pylons were erected by dragging the stone blocks up ramps of mud-brick and earth. The outer pylon (*center*) was never completed, and part of the ramp structure remains on the inner wall of the south pylons.

The temples were placed at the edge of the fertile Nile valley. Materials were transported by river and brought to Karnak by canal. The tombs of the pharaohs were located safely away from the floodplain of the river.

Avenue of Sphinxes
The avenue approaching the outer pylon from the ancient canal quayside is lined with stone sphinxes. The effigy of the god Amun was ceremonially escorted in solemn procession along the avenue onto awaiting barges and taken on a periodic pilgrimage to other sacred temple sites.

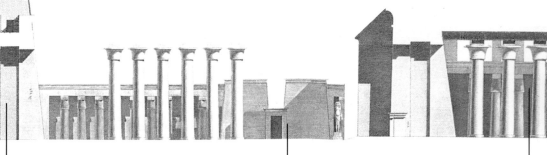

OUTER PYLON
The 140-foot- (42.6-meter-) high outer pylon was once fitted with timber masts bearing immense pennant flags, marking the entrance to the temple.

OUTER COURT
The outer court contains the Kiosk of Taharka, which, used for public ceremonies, marked the limit of public access within the precinct.

HYPOSTYLE HALL
The hypostyle hall consisted of 122 columns, with a central aisle of 12 columns 72 feet (22 meters) high.

RAMSES II

Ramses II was the third king of the 19th Dynasty of Egypt. His 67-year reign (1304–1237 BC) marked the last peak of Egypt's imperial power and was the second longest reign in Egyptian history. Ramses's reputation as a great king rested on both his fame as a soldier and his prowess in war, and his battle feats were well documented throughout Egypt and Nubia. Following defeat at the Battle of Kadesh in the early years of his reign, Ramses led many successful attacks, both to recover lost provinces and to conquer new ones. He also undertook a vast building program, including construction of a number of temples and completion of both the great hypostyle hall at Karnak and two of the six magnificent temples carved out of the cliff at Abu Simbel, one of which was dedicated to his first and favorite queen, Nefertari.

CENTRAL AXIS
The principal halls and courtyards are arranged along a central axis, though the precinct was laterally extended with additional gateways, ceremonial buildings, and commemorative structures.

CONSTRUCTION
The building was gradually filled with earth, providing a platform on which to erect the stone blocks and beams. On completion, the building was then excavated to reveal the internal volume.

Hypostyle Hall
The great hypostyle hall was once covered by a stone roof and lit along its raised, central aisle by a clerestory pierced by stone grilles. The aisle is flanked by 12 main columns 12 feet (3.6 meters) in diameter. To either side are seven rows of nine columns, which recede into the darkness, producing an effect of limitless space.

OBELISK OF HATSHEPSUT
The 95-foot- (29-meter-) high obelisk, originally plated with gold, was transported to the site by barge, raised with ramps and levers into a pit of sand, and lowered onto its locating plinth.

Life within the temple was regulated by the rising and setting of the sun, the cycles of the planets, and the flooding of the Nile. The ceremonial rites and creation and immortalization beliefs use the imagery of darkness and light, symbolized in the alternation of dark interiors with bright courtyards.

SPECIFICATION

•*Location*	Karnak, Egypt
•*Date*	1530–323 BC
•*Height of hypostyle hall*	78 ft (24 m)
•*Building structure*	Stone
•*Building type*	Temple

SACRED LAKE
The artificial lake was used for the daily rituals of bathing and ablution undertaken by the priesthood. It also provided a breeding ground for the birds sacrificed as offerings in the temple.

INNER COURTYARD
Successive pylon gateways, flanked by obelisks, provide access to the inner courtyard.

SANCTUARY
The sanctuary contains the sacred effigy of Amun, placed in a boat, ritually bathed, anointed, and brought offerings of food.

BOTANICAL HALL
The oldest part of the temple includes the botanical hall of Thutmose III, with walls decorated with every known species of flora and fauna in his kingdom.

THE PARTHENON

THE PARTHENON (447–432 BC) by Ictinus and Callicrates is situated on the summit of the Acropolis in Athens. Perhaps the greatest monument of the Hellenic period (650–323 BC), it summarizes the ultimate refinement of the Doric temple. The rectangular plan measures 102 x 226 feet (31 x 69 meters). The *peristyle*, the range of 8 by 17 columns surrounding the temple, contains two rooms, enclosed within solid, ashlar walls. The larger room, or *naos*, with its inner, supporting colonnade, accommodated the statue of the patron goddess, Athena. The local, white Pentelic marble provided the perfect medium for the sharpness of detail required by the design and for the sculpted relief panels of the frieze and portico. The building was subject to meticulous refinements of proportion and geometry, known as *entasis*, to maintain an appearance of exact alignment. Apparently perpendicular and horizontal lines are, in fact, set out within curved and inclining planes, to correct the optical illusion of perspective distortion.

PERICLES

Pericles (ca. 495–429 BC), a fifth-century Athenian statesman, was the leader of Athens from about 450 until his death. Under Pericles, Greek architecture and sculpture reached their highest point. He is best remembered for his wide-ranging program of public building, in which he commissioned numerous sacred and public buildings.

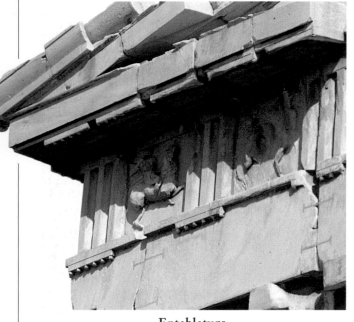

Entablature
The columns are topped by a wide capital and a slab of stone called an abacus, which helps to relieve the tensile forces in the beam. The Greek form of construction employed a simple post-and-beam (trabeated) arrangement, translated into stone from ancient principles developed in timber construction.

SPECIFICATION

- **Location**   Athens, Greece
- **Date**   447–432 BC
- **Architects**   Ictinus and Callicrates
- **Building structure**   Stone and Pentelic marble
- **Building type**   Temple

END COLUMNS
The end columns have a closer spacing and thicker diameter than the main columns and incline diagonally toward the center of the temple to counteract their appearance of outward inclination. The other columns are inclined inward, 2.4 inches (6 centimeters) from the vertical.

DORIC ORDER
The columns have the monumental proportions of the Doric Order. The drums of white Pentelic marble were carved *in situ* to their fluted profiles, which deepen toward the top to emphasize the shadow lines and volumetric composition.

The Parthenon Frieze
The marble panels depict scenes from the procession of the Athenian Knights, contests between the gods and mythical figures, heroic battles of the Greeks and the Amazons, and scenes from the siege of Troy. The frieze's main subject (shown here) is the procession of worshipers on their way to the Acropolis to celebrate the festival called the Great Panathenaea in honor of the goddess Athena. The frieze panels were removed from the building between 1801 and 1803.

The Acropolis
The sacred and defensive site of the Acropolis contains some of the most impressive monuments of the Greek period. It has served as a model of an idealized civic society for Western architecture.

ENTABLATURE
The entablature is composed of lintels connected by bow-tie-shaped iron clamps. The lintels have a faceted, curved profile, rising 2.4 inches (6 centimeters) toward the center.

FRIEZE
The marble frieze was carved along the top of the inner entablature of the *naos* wall just below the peristyle ceiling.

The Statue of Athena
The naos *was dominated by the statue of the patron goddess, Athena, by the sculptor Phidias. Lit by the rising sun from the central, east-facing doorway, the statue, constructed from plates of gold and ivory, stood 42 feet (12.8 meters) high.*

STEPS
The steps have a curved profile, rising toward the center. The treads are set with a slight upward tilt. The devices of perspective correction produce a complex geometry for construction.

The high-relief sculptures of the frieze are cut more deeply toward the top of the panels to correct the apparent foreshortening when viewed from below.

ENTASIS
The tapering columns are swollen in section about two-fifths of the way up, to correct the illusion of a concave profile that a straight-sided shaft would produce.

THE COLOSSEUM

THE ROMAN EMPEROR VESPASIAN commissioned this vast amphitheater as a grand civic gesture to satisfy the escalating public appetite for spectacular shows of violent entertainment. The Colosseum (AD 70–82) in Rome was a public reminder of the power and organization of the Roman Empire. Games were staged in increasingly elaborate spectacles, to which combatants, victims, and animals were imported from across the empire. Up to 5,000 pairs of gladiators and 5,000 animals were slaughtered in a single event before 50,000 spectators. The popularity of Emperors was judged by the success of their games, which continued until the collapsing empire lacked the resources to stage them. The Colosseum's program of rapid construction taxed the organizational skill and ingenuity of the builders, who used shift work, prefabrication, modular building, elaborate machinery, and a largely skilled workforce in methods not unfamiliar in 20th-century projects.

The name "Colosseum" derives not from the scale of the building but from the nearby colossal statue of Nero, which was erected within the grounds of the preexisting Golden House of Nero.

CORBELED BRACKETS
Corbeled brackets can be seen on the upper level, which once supported timber masts and a large canvas awning (later made from embroidered silk). It was used to shade the seats exposed to direct sunlight.

Seating Levels
The tiered structure of the seating levels is supported by load-bearing masonry walls and outer piers radiating from the center. This system enabled building material to be raised along the inclined sections and supported on scaffolding platforms with workers at each tier, permitting a greater pace of construction.

PIERS
Eighty massive piers support the outer wall, which is connected to the inner piers and walls by concrete vaults.

SPECIFICATION

- **Location** — Rome, Italy
- **Date** — AD 70–82
- **Height** — 157.5 ft (48 m)
- **Building structure** — Stone, brick, and concrete
- **Building type** — Civic arena

It has been calculated that the construction of the external walls alone would have required 292,000 cartloads of travertine stone to build – brought along a specially constructed road from Tivoli.

THREE-QUARTER COLUMNS
The three-quarter columns on the outer walls are included purely as decoration, rising through the ascending tiers with their Orders roughly derived from Greek architecture.

In addition to the gladiatorial combats, criminals were executed under sentence of exposure to wild beasts, and mythological and historical battles were enacted with combatants dressed in theatrical costume.

EMPEROR VESPASIAN

Vespasian (Titus Flavius Vespasianus) (AD 9–79) was Roman Emperor from AD 69 to 79. Born in Italy of humble origin, he completed a governorship in Africa (AD 63–66) and also led triumphant campaigns in Palestine (AD 67–68). Following Nero's death in AD 68, Vespasian became founder of the Flavian dynasty and was declared emperor the following year. His consolidation of the empire, together with policies of public reform, brought political stability, and he embarked on a vast building program. In addition to beginning the Colosseum, Vespasian built his Forum and the Temple of Peace (AD 71–79).

Construction Materials
The materials of construction vary according to their imposed loads. Stone of higher strength was used for the piers at the outer walls, with lighter brick and masonry closer to the arena. Concrete (see p. 14) was used extensively for construction of the vaulted floors and encircling corridors.

Spectators
The auditorium accommodated 50,000 spectators in rising tiers of seats, which were allocated by ticket in sections according to rank. The arena mirrored the hierarchy of Roman society. The Emperor and his retinue sat in elevated ringside seats; in the upper levels sat slaves, foreigners, and women.

INAUGURATION GAMES
The building was completed in a remarkably short period. The first games were held in AD 80, although the upper story may have been incomplete.

The immense fabric awning (velarium), winched into position by gangs of sailors, shaded the spectators from the intense summer heat.

WALLS
Originally covered with stucco, the walls reveal their structure of travertine stone blocks laid in courses on mortar beds secured by lead and bronze clamps. The upper sections are of lighter brickwork and tufa limestone.

Travertine stone bollards set into the pavement at a slight incline may have provided anchorage and hauling blocks for the pulley system needed to raise the awning.

EXITS
The many *vomitoria* (exits) provided access to the staircases serving the upper levels. From this remarkably efficient design, it is estimated that a capacity crowd of 50,000 could exit in three minutes. The consecutive numbering above the entrance arches indicates the seat positions.

SITUATION
The Colosseum stands on the site of the lake of the former Golden House of Nero. The lake was drained by a main sewer, discharging into the Tiber River.

COLLAPSED WALLS
Large sections of the walls have collapsed or have been removed. Following the demise of the games, the site was used as a source of building material, reclaimed for many projects throughout Rome.

Sections of floor could be removed to flood the entire arena with water to a depth of 5 feet (1.5 meters) to stage mock naval battles.

THE PANTHEON

THE SUCCESSIVE PERIODS of the Roman Empire provided a continuity of architectural development that advanced techniques in construction and engineering. Although indebted to the established Orders of Greek architecture, the Romans were to find a new form of expression in the range of their building types, their spatial complexity, and a coordinated urban-planning program that achieved cohesion throughout the empire. The structural potential of the true arch, previously utilized in Etruscan architecture, found its logical conclusion in the Roman vault and dome. They, in turn, provided an opportunity for new architectural forms, exceeding the limitations of Greek post-and-beam (trabeated) construction. Systematic engineering methods were used to exploit local resources and to manufacture materials. Domed, concrete-shell construction was used in one of the most impressive surviving buildings of the Roman period, the Pantheon (AD 120–24) in Rome. Uniquely preserved by virtue of its transformation into a church in the 7th century, its astonishing 142-foot- (43.4-meter-) span was unequaled until the 19th century.

Portico
The Pantheon incorporates part of the portico from a preceding temple. This caused confusion in the dating and attribution of the building. However, suppliers' marks stamped on the rotunda's brickwork confirmed the construction date as being within the early part of Emperor Hadrian's rule (AD 117–38).

SPECIFICATION

- *Location*   Rome, Italy
- *Date*   AD 120–24
- *Span of dome* 142 ft (43.4 m)
- *Building structure* Brick, stone, and concrete
- *Building type* Temple
- *Construction time* 4 years

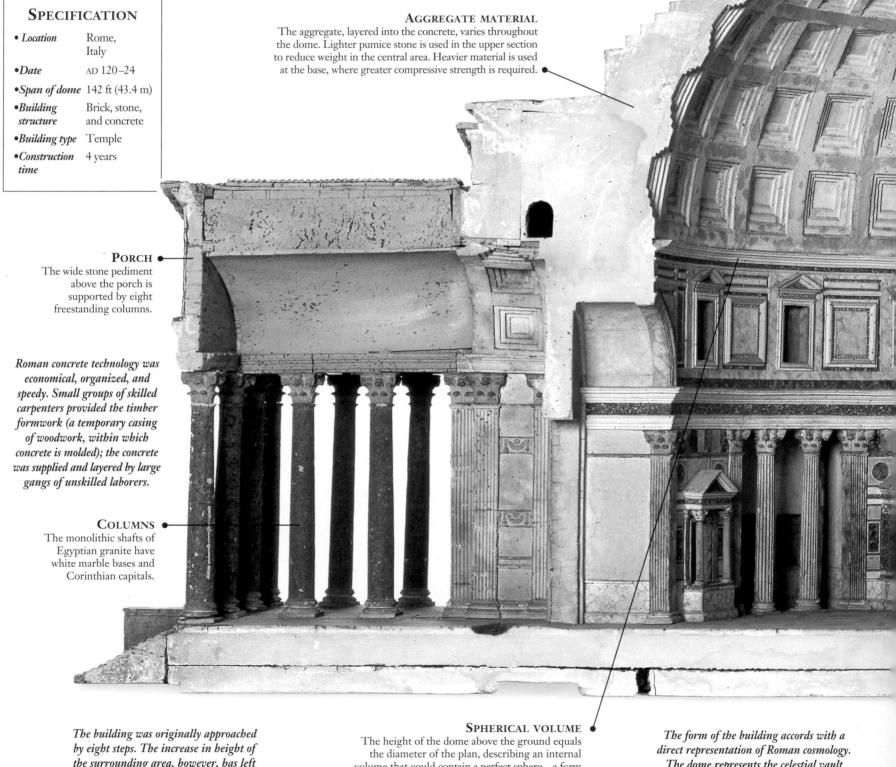

AGGREGATE MATERIAL
The aggregate, layered into the concrete, varies throughout the dome. Lighter pumice stone is used in the upper section to reduce weight in the central area. Heavier material is used at the base, where greater compressive strength is required.

PORCH
The wide stone pediment above the porch is supported by eight freestanding columns.

Roman concrete technology was economical, organized, and speedy. Small groups of skilled carpenters provided the timber formwork (a temporary casing of woodwork, within which concrete is molded); the concrete was supplied and layered by large gangs of unskilled laborers.

COLUMNS
The monolithic shafts of Egyptian granite have white marble bases and Corinthian capitals.

The building was originally approached by eight steps. The increase in height of the surrounding area, however, has left the building in a shallow depression.

SPHERICAL VOLUME
The height of the dome above the ground equals the diameter of the plan, describing an internal volume that could contain a perfect sphere – a form of particular cosmological significance.

The form of the building accords with a direct representation of Roman cosmology. The dome represents the celestial vault illuminated by the central source of the sun.

Relieving Arches
Brick arches, embedded in the structure of the wall, act as internal buttresses, distributing the loads from the dome to the walls. Brickwork was commonly used in walls, arches, vaults, and domes. In buildings of importance, the brick was faced with a hard, stucco render and, more lavishly, with a sophisticated arrangement of stone and marble cladding, applied in panels to the brickwork and restrained by bronze cramps and pins.

EMPEROR HADRIAN

Hadrian (AD 76–138) was Roman emperor from AD 117. He was a great admirer of Greek culture and a patron of the arts. As well as for his political achievements, Hadrian was renowned as a poet and an architectural designer. Among his buildings, were the Villa at Tivoli (AD 124), outside Rome, and the Temple of Venus (AD 135) in Rome, built largely to his own design.

COFFERED CEILING
The form of the coffers emphasizes the lower, recessed moldings, helping to compensate for the perspective distortion when viewed from the ground.

CONCRETE
During construction, the dome was supported on timber formwork until the concrete had set.

ROOF LINE
The building is a three-tiered cylinder covered by a hemispherical dome. The thickening of material at the dome's perimeter counteracts its outward thrust.

It was the Romans who introduced concrete, a building material that offered the potential for large, spanning, monolithic shell structures for domes and vaults. Their concrete consisted of lime mixed with volcanic soil, known as Pozzolana. It was applied in layers with an aggregate material, such as broken roof tiles, between the faces of brickwork that formed the inner and outer skins. Unlike contemporary concrete, it was not reinforced and required external buttressing, making it unsuitable for restraining tensile loads. In addition, it was not as fluid when mixed, limiting the complexity of the formwork shapes.

Ocular Window
The center of the dome is pierced by a 26-foot- (8-meter-) diameter ocular window, open to the sky – the only source of light. This helps reduce the central weight of the construction and obviates the structural difficulty of placing window openings in the perimeter. The effect is dramatic, giving a sense of simplicity and unity.

PATTERNED FLOOR
The floor is paved with colored flags of marble, porphyry, and granite. The square and circular checkerboard pattern complements the ceiling coffers.

NICHES
Niches set within the thickness of the wall were dedicated to the five planets known to the Romans, and to the luminaries, the sun and the moon.

RESTRAINING CUPOLAS
Above the niches are restraining cupolas, which help relieve the stresses at the edge of the dome and translate the loads vertically, via the walls, to the foundations.

ISE SHRINE

THE SACRED SHRINES at Ise Jingu on Ise Bay, southern Honshu, Japan, preserve the ancient traditions of Japan's indigenous Shinto beliefs. The main complex comprises two separate shrines, each enclosed by four wooden fences. The Imperial Shrine, also known as the Inner Shrine, is dedicated to Amaterasu Omikami, the sun goddess, from whom the Japanese imperial family traces its descent. The Outer Shrine is dedicated to Toyouke Okami, the goddess of farming and harvest. At both shrines, the central enclosure that houses the main shrine, or *shoden*, is flanked by structures that provide storage and accommodation for guardians and officiates. The sacred compound, which the public cannot enter, is destroyed and rebuilt on alternating sites at 20-year intervals. Practiced since AD 690, this traditional process of renewal, *shikinen sengu*, allows the precise skills of timber joinery in each rebuilding to be undertaken by three successive generations of craftsmen. This remarkable building provides a rare view of the crisp detail and powerful simplicity much admired in Japanese architecture.

With its meticulous and disciplined structure, formal simplicity, and spiritual presence, the Ise Shrine embodies the essence of Japanese architecture in the same way that the Parthenon (see p. 10) can be seen to exemplify Western architectural attitudes.

Decorative Fittings
The doors are decorated with metal brackets, introduced in subsequent rebuilding. Other elements, such as the colored balls mounted on the balustrade posts, illustrate Chinese architectural influences that arrived with the introduction of Buddhism in the 6th century AD.

WEST AND EAST TREASURIES
The western treasury houses ceremonial regalia, while the eastern treasury contains silks and paper. These separate buildings flank the *shinden*, in which the ancestral deity is enshrined.

SPECIFICATION	
•*Location*	Honshu, Japan
•*Date*	2nd century AD
•*Building structure*	Timber-frame
•*Building type*	Temple
•*Construction time*	Rebuilt every 20 years

The compound is reconstructed on alternating adjacent sites at 20-year intervals, allowing each rebuilding to be undertaken by three generations of craftsmen, overseeing, executing, or apprenticed to the construction.

COLUMNS
The supporting columns are embedded in the ground. After the dismantling of the structure for periodic rebuilding, the central "heart pillar," which has a particular spiritual significance, remains *in situ* until reincorporated into the next rebuilding of the site.

SHRINE
The shrine contains objects belonging to the emperor, including a comb and a mirror. His investment ceremony is held in the privacy of the shrine.

SHINTO

The indigenous religion of Japan, Shinto is centered on the worship of nature and the veneration of the spirits of nature – *kami* – found in mountains, rocks, trees, and other natural features. Shinto shrines dedicated to *kami* are found across Japan, particularly in areas of natural beauty. Respect is traditionally shown at these sites by placing offerings, as here at these *meota-iwa* (wedded rocks) near Ise.

Chigi

The forked finials, or chigi, on the ridge of the frame have become highly stylized, evolving beyond their structural purpose of support into decorative and ritualized elements of construction. The finials are derived from a method of traditional joinery used to secure timber frames. Their use was later restricted to buildings of cultural significance and noble patronage. The building's continual replication has tended toward an exaggeration of iconographic elements.

METALLIC CAPS

Embellishing the ends of the frame, metallic caps protect the exposed grain of the timber, which is where it is most vulnerable to moisture penetration and decay.

RIDGE BILLETS

The ridge billets, or *katsuogi*, restrain the ridge boards and help anchor the traditional roof thatch of miscanthus grass. The ridge is supported by two centrally placed cypress posts in a construction system that has survived from about the 2nd century AD. The shrine is thought to have achieved its final form in the 6th century.

Tiered Fencing

Four concentric fences protect the sacred inner compound from public view. Access for worship is severely restricted to priests, officiates, and members of the imperial family. Traditionally, the kami have been worshiped in sacred and forbidden areas, such as forests and mountains.

RAISED PLATFROM

The raised platform of the building is derived from the ancient form of rice storehouses, which were raised above the ground to protect food from vermin and flooding.

SHODEN

The building is entered by a covered porch. The main *shoden* measures 35 x 18 feet (10.8 x 5.4 meters), comprising a main timber frame of three bays wide and two bays deep.

WALLS

The walls are formed from timber planks, horizontally fitted into rebated channels in the main vertical framing posts. The structure is surrounded by a covered veranda.

SANTA SOPHIA

THE ROMAN METHODS of organized labor and engineering, combined with the assimilation of indigenous traditions, were celebrated in the scale and magnificence of Santa Sophia (AD 532–37), the most important church of the Byzantine Empire. This monumental building has a vast central nave, measuring 225 x 107 feet (68.6 x 32.6 meters), crowned by a ribbed dome of brick and stone. The interior, lined with colored marbles and lustrous mosaics, achieves a remarkable quality of natural lighting. Externally, the building presents a complex arrangement of piers and cupolas, which are supported by monumental and unadorned bearing walls and buttresses. The minarets were added following its conversion to a mosque in 1453. Despite the concealment and disfigurement of much of the original decoration, this awesome structure communicates much of the ethereal mystery and power of the Byzantine world.

Interior Galleries
The interior galleries are supported by columns with monolithic (single-piece) shafts of exotic, colored marble. The capitals and arcades are highly detailed and are carved with tracery motifs incorporating the monogram of Emperor Justinian I.

PROFILE ●
The shallow central dome was severely damaged following an earthquake in AD 557 and was rebuilt using a higher profile of greater stability.

MINARETS ●
After over 900 years as a consecrated church, in –1453, following the capture of Constantinople by the Turks, the building was converted into a mosque, and minaret towers were added.

"[The dome] seems not to rest upon solid masonry, but to cover the space with its golden dome suspended from Heaven"
PROCOPIUS

JUSTINIAN I

After the Roman Empire converted to Christianity, Constantinople became the capital in AD 330. Justinian I (ca. 482–565) was Byzantine emperor from AD 527 to 565 and is renowned for his contribution to architecture. In addition to Santa Sophia, Justinian's program of building included aqueducts, bridges, and fortifications along the frontiers of the Byzantine Empire.

The building was erected in a remarkably short period of five years. Two teams of 5,000 workmen competed with each other in the building of the east and west sections.

BUTTRESSING ●
Earthquakes have caused significant movement within the building, requiring extensive buttressing and additional support structures.

Nave Interior
The central section of the nave is spanned by a vast central dome 107 feet (32.6 meters) in diameter. Natural light penetrates apertures at the base of the dome and windows placed within the tympanum wall.

Denied the local availability of pozzolana cement, the Roman builders were unable to use the technique of concrete construction that had facilitated the building of single-domed structures, such as the Pantheon. However, a method of brick-skin construction, using thickened layers of mortar, produced some of the advantages of speedy construction, deploying large gangs of comparatively unskilled labor.

CONSTRUCTION
The scale of the dome was limited by the precedent of the dome of the Pantheon, which had established the constructional limit of a monolithic dome. Following Santa Sophia's collapse, it was rebuilt to a higher profile, and additional height and mass were given to the buttressing towers.

CENTRAL DOME
The central dome is braced by the eastern and western hemispherical domes, which, together, form the main nave.

WINDOWS
The presence of clerestory windows at this point would seem to contradict the requirement for mass to resist the outward thrust of the dome. But the windows actually reduce the risk of cracking, enabling the dome to perform efficiently as a massive shell.

SPRINGING ARCHES
The springing arches and piers provide the primary route of transference to the ground of loads imposed by the main domes.

SPECIFICATION

- *Location*   Istanbul, Turkey
- *Date*   AD 532–37
- *Height*   180 ft (54.8 m)
- *Building structure*   Brick and stone
- *Building type*   Church/Mosque

TOWERS
Towers abut the north and south elevations on either side of the springing arches that support the central dome. The mass of the towers resists the side thrusts exerted from the relieving arches.

TYMPANUM WALL
The tympanum wall, beneath the main relieving arches, is theoretically non-load-bearing and thus is able to provide maximum window area to illuminate the interior.

PIERS
The main piers are constructed from stone, rather than mortar-bonded brick, which requires a substantial curing period before achieving its bonded strength. The use of stone for the initial construction phase enabled work to proceed at a faster pace.

TEMPLE I, TIKAL

RISING ABOVE THE CANOPY OF THE RAIN FOREST, the pyramidal towers of the Mayan city of Tikal dominate the landscape. The Mayan civilization flourished during the Classic period between AD 300 and 900, but declined abruptly, its great cities abandoned 500 years before the Spanish conquest of South America in the 16th century. Tikal lies in the Petén region of Guatemala in Central America. Excavations have uncovered groups of platforms and stone structures dispersed across a 26.5-square-mile (68.6-square-kilometer) site. At the center of this city, with its wide causeways connecting specific building clusters, is a stucco-lined plaza measuring 280 x 220 feet (85 x 67 meters). Facing each other across this platform are two towers, the larger known as Temple I, or the Temple of the Great Jaguar (ca. AD 500). The building groups share a geomantic relationship, suggesting an urban hierarchy and a solar and astral alignment. The interiors of the temples are small and simple. Elevated high above the plaza, they indicate an elitist ceremonial purpose hidden from the assembled crowds below. The urban center, with an estimated population at its height of around 50,000, was sustained by the support of a wide agricultural empire, which had cultural links with distant cities of the same period. These monuments, now isolated among the dense tangle of undergrowth, communicate silently of a mysterious and lost culture.

ROOF COMB
The temple is surmounted by an intricately carved and painted crenellated ridge of a much greater height than the temple vault. It rises from the rear wall and provides an imposing silhouette to the structure.

SCULPTURAL DECORATION
The external face of the temple vault carries sculptural decoration depicting a large, seated figure and serpent.

SANCTUARY
The temple sanctuary comprises three connected chambers with a corbel-vaulted roof. The purpose of the sanctuary is connected with the frequent rites of human sacrifice. The victim's blood ran onto the steps, and the still-beating heart was ripped out and offered to the gods. The inner face of the wooden lintel above the opening is carved with an image of a jaguar.

TERRACES
The pyramid rises in nine tiers to a total height of 156 feet (47.5 meters). The distinct terraces represent the mythical levels of the underworld.

The sealed burial chamber contains the remains of the great King Ah Cacau, dating from AD 720. The wealth of ceremonial regalia indicates a king of great importance.

RITUAL ACTIVITIES

This jaguar-shaped bowl from Guatemala, part of the Mayan Empire, may have been used to collect blood offerings. The drawing of blood from one's body often preceded important ceremonies and sacrifices. These ritual activities were complex and intense, with animals, birds, flowers, jade, and blood being sacrificed in return for divine favor. Special ceremonies took place on the Mayan New Year's Day, with each successive month being devoted to a particular god. Each social group, from priests to fishermen, celebrated its own religious feast.

Panoramic View of the Temples

The clusters of pyramidal temples are elevated on high, terraced plinths and arranged around large civic spaces and smaller courtyards. The city lies, roughly, along a broken ridge, connected by a series of causeways that may have been surrounded by reservoirs, providing food and access to the isolated site. Temple I (right) faces the Temple of the Mask. The northern acropolis and standing stones can be seen in the distance.

STEPS
The temple is approached by a steep flight of steps. The stairs now visible were used during the construction; the original ceremonial flight (now deteriorated) was much wider.

ASHLAR STONE
The pyramid has a rubble and concrete core faced with blocks of ashlar stone set in regular mortar courses.

Stone Tablets

Knowledge of Mayan culture has been partly deciphered from the detailed carvings on the upright stone tablets (stelae) found throughout the city – in particular, stones found in an axial arrangement on the Great Plaza. The stelae record a complex and precise calendar of dynastic events. The calendar has a cyclical structure, divided into 20-year intervals; this event was recorded by the construction of a form of pyramid structure.

BALL COURT
Adjacent to the foot of the tower is a ball court for contests between opposing teams. A ball was driven through a stone hoop using elbows and hips.

SPECIFICATION

- **Location** Tikal, Guatemala, Central America
- **Date** ca. AD 500
- **Height** 156 ft (47.5 m)
- **Building structure** Stone, concrete, and rubble core
- **Building type** Temple pyramid

KANDARIYA MAHADEV TEMPLE, KHAJURAHO

KHAJURAHO IN CENTRAL INDIA includes over 80 structures, all built during the relatively short period between about AD 950 and 1050. The temples, of which only 24 survive, were commissioned by the Chandella kings for their capital city in a style conflating all the temple-building traditions of the late Hindu period. The temples, which were once surrounded by irrigated lakes, fell into disuse after the dynasty ended in the 12th century and were abandoned to the encroaching jungle for seven centuries until systematic excavations were undertaken in 1906. Each temple accommodates a devotional image in the darkened, vaulted sanctuary, situated beneath the elaborately carved tower. The sandstone surfaces are filled with decoration in horizontal, laminated tiers, rising through the adjoining *mandapa* (hall) to the height of the main *sikhara* (tower). Continuous friezes of figures carved in deep relief create a highly animated pageant of warriors, dancers, elephants, acrobats, horses, musicians, hunters, and lovers in erotic embrace. The temples at Khajuraho are among the most notable examples of Hindu architecture in Central India.

Sacred Mountain
The dominant tower, surrounded by smaller peaks, derives from the sacred image of Mount Meru – the "world mountain." This is a representation of the mountain home of the mythical gods of Indra, which formed the focus of the world's spiritual axis. The Khajuraho temples were shared by the Saiva, Vaishnava, and Jaina sects.

MAIN SIKHARA
The main *sikhara* (tower) is 117 feet (35.6 meters) above the ground on a 13-foot- (4-meter-) high plinth. The shrines, though relatively small in dimension, have a remarkable monumentality of composition.

MINIATURE TOWERS
The main *sikhara* is composed of ascending tiers of 85 miniature versions of the main tower, arranged into a commanding and unified design.

TRANSEPTS
Lateral transepts with canopied balconies emerge on both north and south sides, opening the interior to cross-ventilation.

Temple Plinth
The base of the temple is constructed from continuous horizontal bands forming a splayed plinth. The rhythmic recession and projection accentuates the light and shadow, adding to the effect of the animated sculptural surface. The tiered bands are decorated with a variety of floral and vegetal moldings.

FIGURES
Most of the figures are between 29 and 35 inches (75–90 centimeters) high and illustrate an astonishing variety of heavenly and earthly images sculpted in superb movement with minute observation of detail.

SCULPTURES
The three repeated bands of sculptures carry 646 divine and temporal figures carved on the outside frieze, with a further 226 figures sculpted inside.

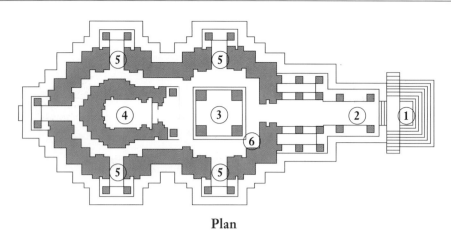

Plan

Each of the temples follows an east–west alignment and is raised on a platform approached by a steep flight of stairs. The areas distinct within the plan are interconnected and are approached in the following sequence: (1) stairs; (2) entrance porch; (3) mandapa; (4) sanctuary and sikhara; (5) lateral transept with balcony; (6) ambulatory.

Erotic Figures
The explicitly erotic subjects are presented with a liveliness and delicacy that deeply shocked the English colonial archaeologists who excavated the site in the early 20th century. Guidebooks at that time discouraged visitors to the site for fear of impropriety and moral corruption.

CHANDELLA KINGS

The Chandella kings were the most powerful rulers of northern and Central India from the 9th to the 12th century, achieving their zenith under the rule of Vidyadhara (1004–35). During his reign, important temples, including Kandariya Mahadev, were constructed. All of them show a remarkable stylistic cohesion. Following his death, the Chandella kingdom declined. Temples continued to be built at Khajuraho until the 11th century.

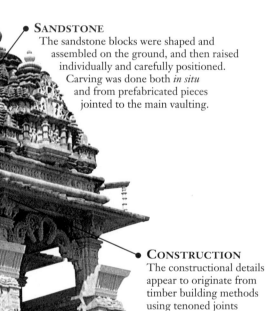

SANDSTONE
The sandstone blocks were shaped and assembled on the ground, and then raised individually and carefully positioned. Carving was done both *in situ* and from prefabricated pieces jointed to the main vaulting.

CONSTRUCTION
The constructional details appear to originate from timber building methods using tenoned joints translated into stone.

Stone Sculptures
The entrance porch is flanked by sculptures of crocodiles springing from the diminutive columns and supported by a multitude of smaller figures, each with a profusion of minutely carved details.

The devotional image is placed in the darkened sanctuary beneath the main tower, which is buttressed by additional towers, entrance vestibule, and hall.

PORTICO
Pilgrims progress from the open portico into increasing darkness within the sanctuary. Light is admitted to the ambulatory via the canopied balconies.

The erotic figures are consistent with the Tantric belief in the primal life energy of sexual coupling, incorporated into religious buildings for its associations with fertility and joy.

SPECIFICATION

•*Location*	Khajuraho, India
•*Date*	ca. 950–1050
•*Height*	117 ft (35.6 m)
•*Length*	109 ft (33.2 m)
•*Building structure*	Stone
•*Building type*	Temple

PISA CATHEDRAL

THE WEALTH AND PRESTIGE of the established centers of Christian worship from the mid-11th to mid-12th century are reflected in the increasing scale of church building. This is illustrated in the world-famous grouping of Romanesque cathedral, campanile, and baptistery in Pisa, Italy. Constructional developments in stone vaulting and the use of the peripheral arcade (helping to reduce the thickness of the external wall) are used to explore the possibilities of light and decoration, realized later to great effect in European Gothic architecture. In Italy, the remains of Roman architecture provided a source of both architectural material and stylistic precedent. Blended with the influences of Byzantine culture, they provided a measure of continuity between the antique and medieval worlds. The simple, rectangular, basilican form of the early Christian church, dating from the 4th century, has a central nave and side aisles, later adapted to ceremonial practices that required crossing transepts, forming a cruciform plan.

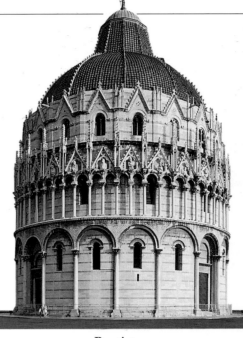

Baptistery
The baptistery (1153–1265) was designed by Dioti Salvi. The unusual profile of the ribbed dome is the product of a composite structural system. The outer dome spans the diameter of the circular baptistery, and an inner cone, which accentuates the height, is supported on an internal colonnade.

Marble Panels
Polychromatic marble panels provide the characteristic decoration on the façade. The Classical Orders of architecture, with Corinthian capitals, are deployed with a crudeness of detail but a richness of decoration.

COLONNADE
The delicacy and articulation of the arcading in the upper sections of the main façade are characteristic of the Italian Romanesque.

GABLE WALL
The rhythmical arcading of the gable wall, together with the polychromatic marble banding, gives Pisa Cathedral its distinctive character.

ROMANESQUE VAULTING

Developments in techniques of stone vaulting began to open out the nave and aisles, introducing spatial variation into the strictly rectilinear plan of the basilican church. The nave at Pisa is relatively confined, since the structural limitations of semicircular vaulting do not allow the span and flexibility possible with the pointed arch and the rib vault (see p. 26). The central crossing did not begin to dominate the plan until further developments produced the centralized plan of the Renaissance (see p. 44).

ARCADE
The arches and columns of the peripheral arcade developed as a Romanesque decorative treatment of the Classical façade.

STRUCTURAL FRAME
The arches and columns emerge as distinctive structural elements within the external façade. The repetition of this simple unit reduces the reliance on a uniformly load-bearing wall. This tendency pointed toward the development of a masonry superstructure – the characteristic device of the later Gothic period.

Nave
The nave is flanked on both sides by aisles used for the display of religious images and chapels dedicated to the saints. This arrangement is achieved through the use of stone vaulting and a colonnade supporting the nave wall.

Apse and Transept
Developments in Christian worship moved the form of the church toward its characteristic cruciform plan and central tower. The apse, originally a niche at the eastern end of the nave, is enlarged, providing a focus for the rites of Mass. The arms of the cross are extended, allowing devotional chapels and the crossing point, which is dominated by a central tower.

DOME
The brick and stone dome was constructed in 1090 and is contemporary with the baptistery in Florence. The arcade that surrounds the dome was completed in 1383.

LEANING TOWER
The tower (1174–1271) leans at an alarming 14 feet (4.2 meters) from top to base and continues at a rate of 1.1 minutes of inclination per decade, which may result in its eventual collapse.

SUBSIDENCE
The lean and subsidence of the tower first became apparent during construction. The top two stories are constructed with a wedge-shaped section in an attempt to counterbalance the accumulated tilt.

CENTRAL CROSSING
The central crossing originally may have been a covered tower, removed to expose the masonry dome, following the fashion of 14th-century Tuscan churches established in Florence.

SPECIFICATION
- **Location**   Pisa, Italy
- **Date**   1063–1118 and 1261–72
- **Building structure**   Brick, stone, and marble
- **Building type**   Cathedral

MARBLE BANDING
The cathedral is decorated with horizontal bands of alternate courses of colored marble, which is characteristic of buildings in central Italy.

Many of the granite columns are of Roman origin. Materials from Classical ruins were frequently incorporated into the construction of new buildings.

BASE
The limited area of the base for the tower's height produced a loading on the foundations that exceeded that of traditional building practices. The tower is subsiding in a rotational movement caused by failure in the clay 33 feet (10 meters) below the surface.

DURHAM CATHEDRAL

ENSHRING THE HOLY RELICS OF ST. CUTHBERT, the cathedral, monastery, and castle in Durham, England, are situated on a promontory high above a loop in the River Wear. This elevated position, together with the rapid pace of the cathedral's early construction (1093–1104), gives a memorable impression of the power and solidity of Norman architecture and the spirit of the Romanesque in Britain. The holy relics ensured the continued importance and wealth of this northern English outpost as a place of Christian pilgrimage. The monastery and castle reinforced the strategic and military role of the cathedral throughout the Middle Ages until the dissolution of the monasteries (1536–40). The cathedral was the first major structure in England to be vaulted entirely in stone, and the pointed vaults that cross the nave and aisles are the earliest recorded examples of rib vaulting, which was to transform the heavy masonry of the Romanesque into the lightness and soaring verticality of the Gothic. The nave has a powerful and impressive character, which balances the solidity of mass with the lofty proportions of the upper arcade and the verticality of the 73-foot- (22.2-meter-) high vault. The chevron, fluted, reticulated, and spiral motifs of Norman decoration are, for the first time, incised into the broad columns, emphasizing their mass and providing an alternating rhythm that imparts a solemn dignity to this masterpiece of Romanesque architecture.

Galilee Chapel
Added in 1175, the chapel has a timber roof and five-aisle arcade supported on slender compound columns of sandstone and Purbeck marble. The simple cushion capital and chevron moldings that decorate the arch soffits are Romanesque in detail, but, in their lightness of structure, provide a delicate contrast to the monumentality of the nave.

The cathedral was one of 30 churches in England that possessed the right of sanctuary. A criminal seeking refuge was afforded protection within for 37 days. If a pardon had not been obtained within this time, the prisoner was sent into exile.

TRANSVERSE RIBS
The transverse ribs occur at alternating positions above the compound columns that divide the nave into rectangular double vaults.

POINTED-RIB VAULT
The nave is vaulted with one of the earliest recorded forms of the pointed-rib vault. The decorated lines of the lofty transverse arches emphasize the size of the nave, enabling a lightness of structure, the style of which was to develop into Gothic vaulting.

DIAGONAL RIBS
Semicircular diagonal ribs spring from twinned corbels below the clerestory. The grinning face of the carved corbeled brackets is in alignment with the alternate positions of the circular columns.

Transverse arch
Central ridge
Semicircular arch

Ribbed Vault

The ribbed vault combines the ease of construction of the semicircular arch with the flexibility of the height and span of the pointed arch. This technique maintains the central ridge height of the nave while freeing the wall for open arcading or clerestory windows, opening out the nave to allow increased natural light.

BUTTRESSES
The thrust of the nave roof is shared between the nave columns and the side aisles. A premature flying buttress is formed by quadrant arches concealed within the aisle roof structure and thickened piers within the wall.

CHOIR

The four bays of the choir at the eastern end of the nave were completed between 1093 and 1104. The vaulting was rebuilt at the end of the 13th century because of structural instability.

A thin line of blue marble, which crosses the nave near the western font, marks the limit of entrance allowed to women during the Middle Ages.

ROSE WINDOW

The rose window at the far eastern end is an addition by the 18th-century architect James Wyatt, who supervised a number of intrusive modifications, including the stripping of moldings from the external stonework.

SPECIFICATION

- **Location** Durham, England
- **Date** 1093–1133
- **Height** 145 ft (44 m)
- **Building structure** Stone
- **Building type** Cathedral
- **Construction time** 40 years

The Chapel of the Nine Altars (1242–80), which once contained the shrine of St. Cuthbert, is at the far end of the nave and forms an additional transept at the eastern end. The gilded green marble shrine was broken up after the dissolution, though the relics of the saint remain buried beneath the chapel floor.

Western Towers

The cathedral is built on a solid foundation of exposed rock high above the River Wear. The western towers adjoin the Galilee Chapel and date from the 13th century, but were rebuilt in 1487 after being struck by lightning. Rising to 145 feet (44 meters), the towers amplify the massing of the cathedral on its elevated site.

ST. CUTHBERT

St. Cuthbert (ca. AD 624–87) is one of the most revered of English saints. After a vision in AD 651, he entered the Northumbrian monastery of Melrose and is credited with many miraculous events. By AD 685, he had become bishop of Lindisfarne, where he was later to be buried. His relics were moved to Durham after Viking raids in the 9th century AD. He was enshrined in the choir and transept of the cathedral, and consecrated in 1104.

COMPOUND COLUMNS

The compound columns continue to support the transverse ribs. They have a sinuous appearance, but are more substantial than the circular columns and carry the greater loads imparted by the ribbed vaulting

Northern Facade

Viewed across the Palace Green, the northern façade of the cathedral reveals the full length of the 470-foot (143-meter) nave. The Gothic Chapel of the Nine Altars and the tomb of St. Cuthbert are situated at the east end of the cathedral (left). The central tower was completed in 1495 with the addition of a final tier. The towers built above the western end of the nave (right) adjoin the Galilee Chapel, which is perched on the cliff edge.

ANGKOR WAT

THE CITY OF ANGKOR in Cambodia was abandoned to the jungle after periodic occupation as the capital of the Khmer civilization, from the 9th century AD to the 13th century. The temple of Angkor Wat is one precinct in a vast site dispersed over a distance of 31 miles (50 kilometers) from east to west. Built on rising ground and surrounded by an artificial moat, the temple is arranged symmetrically on tiered platforms that ascend to the central tower, which rises to a height of 213 feet (65 meters). Long colonnades connect the towers at each stepped level in concentric rings of rectilinear galleries. The site is approached across the moat, via a stone causeway lined with stone figures. The ascending towers represent the spiritual world and mountain homes of the gods and were probably built in homage to ancestral deities. Artifacts taken from the site and large sections cast from the temple buildings were exhibited in Paris in 1867, announcing a great and unknown civilization rivaling in sophistication the Western achievements of Classical and Gothic architecture.

VISHNU

The original Khmer builders of the 12th century may have erected the temple in honor of ancestral gods. Vishnu, one of the most important Hindu deities, is revered as the protector of the world and restorer of moral order. He is essentially known through a series of 10 reincarnations, known as *avatars*, who appear to protect good or prevent evil on the earth. The most important of these are Rama, fearless and noble upholder of the law, and Krishna, who is associated with altruistic love. Vishnu holds in his hands symbols of creation, domination, universal purity, and knowledge of the power of the mind.

SPECIFICATION

- **Location** — Angkor, Cambodia
- **Date** — 12th century
- **Height** — 213 ft (65 m)
- **Building structure** — Stone
- **Building type** — Temple

The Khmer builders accomplished ambitious religious and civil engineering projects with astonishing accuracy. A 40-mile- (65-kilometer-) long canal was built in virtually a straight line, and a 2-mile- (3-kilometer-) long moat deviates by only 2 inches (5 centimeters) from true alignment.

CENTRAL TOWER

The tower at the center of the third platform forms the focus of the tiered levels. This central sanctuary is linked to the outer tiers by pavilion towers and covered porticos.

MASONRY BONDING

Despite the competence of Khmer builders, much of the stonework is constructed without offset joints between courses. This lack of simple bonding resulted in the subsequent collapse of the masonry.

LOW COLONNADES

The long colonnades form peripheral galleries that connect the main towers. The gallery walls are lined with stone relief carvings depicting female deities and epic scenes.

Although the city of Angkor was abandoned by the Khmer rulers, the temple precinct was continually visited by Buddhist and Hindu pilgrims from as far as Japan, China, and Thailand.

CAUSEWAY

The raised platforms are approached across a wide stone causeway. The form of the balustrade on either side represents the serpent of Hindu mythology – a recurrent image in the myth of creation.

Water

The moat surrounding the temple was supplied by watercourses directed from a river and used for irrigating the land. The Khmers' ability to conserve and direct the supply of water ensured the continual productivity of the land, creating a prosperous and organized society.

TOWERS

The stone towers have roofs formed by corbeling stone blocks in successive tiers. The internal soffits were ground away *in situ* to produce the effect of vaulting. The ceilings were occasionally lined with gilded timber.

Stone Construction

The buildings are constructed chiefly of stone, with detailed bas-reliefs carved into the walls; the corbeled block work and pseudo-vaulted towers are covered with highly animated figures carved into the sandstone and volcanic rock. The construction methods developed by the Khmers show a change from timber to brick and stone. Decorative motifs, such as roof vaults and wall panels (an imitation of bamboo screens), have petrified earlier forms of construction.

TEMPLE MOUNTAIN

The tiered platforms, culminating in a central tower, conform to the *Linga*, or earthly mountain form of temple, representing the sacred Mount Meru of Indian mythology.

STYLISTIC INFLUENCES

In early reconstructions, French archaeologists emphasized the stylistic influences of China, India, and Egypt, wrongly supposing the construction to be by a foreign, rather than an indigenous, civilization.

VAULTED GALLERIES

The curved roof of the galleries is vaulted in corbeled stone blocks, but the form is carved to imitate the overlapping courses of roof tiles.

KRAK DES CHEVALIERS

HIGH ABOVE THE ORONTES VALLEY, defending the Homs Pass in Syria, the Krak des Chevaliers provided a strategic outpost for the military incursions of the crusading knights. Its formidable situation, along with fortifications undertaken in the early 13th century, made it virtually impregnable to attack. Built on the site of a preexisting fort, the castle had three lines of defense – two concentric tiers of fortifications and a final donjon tower (strong, central tower). Though virtually impregnable, its fortification and controlled entrance made it reliant on defensive methods, as it was very difficult for its defenders to mount a counterattack. Krak des Chevaliers was occupied from 1142 by the Knights Hospitaller and was besieged 12 times during their occupation, finally being taken by Berber forces in 1271. Rebuilding and further modifications have maintained the castle as an impressive example of medieval military architecture, indebted in construction techniques to the traditions of Norman masons and the historic fortifications of Arab towns. The castle remained in occupation until the resiting of the village that occupied the interior in 1932.

Vaulted Loggia
The inner courtyard has a vaulted loggia running the length of the banqueting hall, providing a shaded retreat from the fierce heat of the day. The courtyard contains the finest rooms in the castle, used as the main apartments of the knights and probably as a refuge from mercenaries garrisoned in the outer walls.

Lines of Defense
Fortifications are arranged in concentric lines of defense – the outer walls defended from the lower ward, and the upper levels of the castle defended from the towers and inner ward. An open moat and cistern within the outer ward were used for water storage. In 1271, Berber forces besieged the castle and gained access to the outer ward but were unable to proceed farther. The siege lasted for a further month before the defending troops capitulated.

BUTTRESS TOWERS
Along their length, the immense stone walls are strengthened by buttress towers, which offer concealed positions for surveillance and defense.

MACHIOCOULIS
The parapet of the outer walls has a vaulted gallery equipped at intervals with narrow chambers, cantilevered from the face of the wall. The protected chambers, or *machiocoulis*, are used to drop stones through openings in the floor in order to prevent attacking forces from undermining or scaling the walls.

WALL BASE
The thickening at the base of the walls helps protect against attack by sappers charged with excavating lower sections and starting a fire to undermine the structure.

While researching his undergraduate thesis in 1909, T. E. Lawrence (Lawrence of Arabia), undertook a tour of the crusader castles. He described Krak des Chevaliers as "the best preserved and most wholly admirable castle in the world."

SLOTTED OPENINGS
The slotted openings are relatively invulnerable to incoming missiles but have wide internal reveals, increasing the defending archer's scope of fire.

KNIGHTS HOSPITALLER

Krak des Chevaliers was occupied in 1109 and garrisoned by the Knights Hospitaller from 1142, during the crusades undertaken by European Christian forces between the 11th and 14th centuries. These military expeditions were intended to recover the Holy Land (the birthplace of Christ) and the routes of pilgrimage from the possession of Muslim rulers. The successes of the First Crusade and the recapture of Jerusalem were not repeated in later expeditions. Despite the crusaders' winning concessions of pilgrimage and access to the Holy Sepulchre, the Holy Land remained under Muslim control.

Ramped Entrance
On the outer eastern wall, a gatehouse gives access to the upper levels via a narrow, vaulted ramp. This confined entrance would expose intruders to attack from openings flanking the wall and roof along the length of its steep approach. The dogleg turn precludes the use of a large battering ram, and the contrast between light and dark adds to the sense of disorientation.

A windmill was positioned on the tower for grinding corn, and the castle was equipped to endure long periods of siege. Vaults beneath the upper courtyard contained immense storehouses for provisions.

UPPER TOWERS
The inner ward, defended by the upper towers, contained the dormitories, banqueting hall, storerooms, chapel, and apartments of the highest-ranking knights.

GLACIS
The upper walls have a glacis (slope) up to 80 feet (24.3 meters) thick, almost as wide as their height. This monumental form of construction provided resistance to earthquakes as well as to assault from undermining and missile attack.

SPECIFICATION

- **Location** — Syria
- **Date** — 11th century
- **Architects** — Remodeled by the Knights Hospitaller
- **Building structure** — Stone
- **Building type** — Castle

Communication between remote fortifications was made possible by carrier pigeon. The use of carrier pigeons was a technique borrowed from Arab practices.

AQUEDUCT
Water was supplied to the castle by an aqueduct. During periods of siege, the castle had a reserve contained in subterranean, vaulted cisterns.

SQUARE TOWER
The square tower dates from 1285. It was rebuilt following the damage caused during the siege and capture in 1271. Circular towers, by contrast, offered the advantage of being defendable all around. Their circular walls were also less vulnerable to assault, battering ram, or undermining.

NOTRE-DAME, PARIS

THE CRUCIFORM PLAN, elevated nave, transept, and tower of the Gothic cathedral were inherited from 11th-century Romanesque churches. However, it was the structural potential and versatility of the pointed arch and the rib vault (see p. 26) that enabled the early Gothic to exceed all precedents. Notre-Dame (1163–ca. 1250) in Paris is a remarkable illustration of the vision and achievement of the medieval world. The desire for increased height required significant developments in constructional methods. The choir, with a keystone at a height of 108 feet (33 meters), was taller than any previous Gothic structure. As construction began on the nave, the height of the vaults increased a further 6 feet (2 meters), and the method of buttressed support to the side galleries soon revealed weaknesses in the structure. The remedial means sought by the 13th-century masons resulted in the use of that characteristic device of Gothic architecture – the flying buttress.

West Facade
The façade balances the verticality of the twin towers, which align to the width of the double side aisles, with the horizontal banding of the decorated galleries. This produces a simple but powerful western elevation, which dominates the square.

SOUTHWEST TOWER
The 226-foot- (69-meter-) high southwest tower supported the famous 15th-century bell. The bell was recast in 1686, it is said, with the addition of gold and precious stones, reputedly accounting for the clear resonance of its sound.

The Romantic Gothic image of the cathedral was advanced in Victor Hugo's novel **The Hunchback of Notre-Dame** *(1831). The revival of interest in the Gothic successfully enabled Hugo to appeal for the cathedral's restoration.*

BUTTRESSING
The height of the nave and the relative slenderness of the wall, an average of 3 feet (1 meter) thick, required supplementary external buttressing to counteract the lateral thrust of the nave vaulting.

Central Portal
The central portal of the entrance façade is flanked by statues depicting the Last Judgment – the redemption of the pious and the damnation of the wicked.

GLASS
Gothic buildings achieved a remarkable delicacy. The rhythmic structural bays provide the supporting masonry frame, allowing the thin membrane walls to become nonstructural and available for large expanses of glass.

PIERS
Following remedial alterations to the structure, the piers of the buttresses were thickened. The mass of material provides stability and a vertical component to lateral forces transferred from the nave vaulting.

Ornamentation

The building is encrusted with statuary and animated detail. The grotesque ornamentation was embellished in the 19th-century restoration supervised by the famous French architect Viollet-le-Duc. Rather than achieve an authentic rebuilding, the restoration sought to present history as a pastiche of all periods, reflecting the 19th-century taste for Gothic fantasy.

CATHEDRAL BUILDERS

With the aid of only elementary drawings and templates, masons supervised and meticulously directed the construction of the great medieval cathedrals of Europe. The practices of intuitive calculation, based largely on simple mathematical ratios and structural precedent, were closely guarded and passed from one generation of masons to the next. Specific site conditions and the insatiable demand for higher and lighter buildings provided the impetus for continual development.

The timber spire, 315 feet (96 meters) high, was destroyed during the Revolution and replaced by the 19th-century restoration (1845–56) conducted by French architect Eugène Viollet-le-Duc.

SPECIFICATION

•*Location*	Paris, France
•*Date*	1163–ca. 1250
•*Height*	300 ft (90 m)
•*Building structure*	Stone and timber
•*Building type*	Cathedral
•*Consruction time*	ca. 87 years
•*Restored*	19th century

SHALLOW TRANSEPT
The cathedral has a remarkably shallow transept, which, even after extension, does not exceed the line of the outer aisles.

CLERESTORY WINDOWS
The clerestory windows of the original nave were enlarged in the 13th century to supplement natural light entering the interior. This was permitted by developments of the structural frame.

FLYING BUTTRESSES
The flying buttresses have two tiers of support. The upper arm contributes to the stability of the wall, counteracting the wind loading experienced at such height. The main thrust of the wall is supported by the lower arm of the buttress.

THE ALHAMBRA

THE MOORS' CONQUEST OF SPAIN, following their invasions in AD 711, led to a period of occupation lasting for almost eight centuries, until their expulsion by Christian forces in 1492. The last bastion of Moorish rule was the city palace of the Alhambra in Granada. The administration of this most western province of Islam emanated from the southern citadels of Granada and Córdoba. Under the Muslims' tolerant rule, Spain became one of the most educated and cultured centers of Europe. The Arab rulers introduced traditional forms of Islamic architecture and irrigation methods into Spain, taming the summer heat to create lush gardens and shaded, airy courtyards. The Alhambra (1238–1358) summarizes the refined pleasures and grace of Moorish culture. Following the expulsion of the Moors and the unification of Spain, Isabella of Castile (1451–1504) and Ferdinand of Aragon (1452–1516) briefly established their palace there. The Alhambra, with its succession of enchanting apartments, exquisitely detailed colonnades, and courtyard gardens, retains its mysterious charm, a reminder of the rich cultural heritage running parallel to the Christian traditions of the European Gothic.

The Fortified Citadel of the Alhambra

The walls of the Alhambra stand out against the mountains of the Sierra Nevada. The palace is essentially a fortified citadel built upon an 11th-century castle. The severity of the external walls contrasts with the decoration of the internal courtyards, which were designed to be viewed from their center. This characteristic of Islamic architecture is in direct contrast to Classical Western composition, which is determined principally by the external view of the façade.

Patio de la Acequia

The rectilinear garden is enclosed by screen walls on the long sides and an arcade at either end. Raised pathways line the central water channel, which is inset with fountains. The courtyard forms part of the Generalife – summer gardens with shaded verandas overlooking the city.

SPECIFICATION

- **Location**   Granada, Spain
- **Date**   1238–1358
- **Building structure**   Brick and stone
- **Building type**   Fortified palace

The courtyard palace is part of an ancient tradition found in Islamic, Classical Roman, and Chinese architecture. The civilizing influence of a recreational space introduces light and gardens into an outwardly austere, fortified building.

● COURTYARD
Pairs of facing staterooms and private apartments, each afforded a degree of privacy, overlook the courtyard. The internal allocation of spaces is ambiguous, allowing flexibility of use.

TRACERY
The fine tracery of the arcades is carved directly into the stucco applied to the vaulting. The ornate carving produces a raised, decorative design, vividly expressed in the chiaroscuro effects created by bright sunlight.

ISLAMIC DECORATION
Islamic decoration is characterized by the proliferation of minutely detailed geometric vegetal and calligraphic motifs, composed into panels, creating a unified field of decoration.

COMPOSITIONAL RHYTHMS
The complex rhythms, established by repeating elements of the arcades, and the arrangement of slender columns into singles, pairs, and groups of three, assist the expansive feel of openness and lightness in the relatively confined courtyard.

LIONS
The stone lions supporting the alabaster basin are an ancient symbol of royal power and are of earlier Romanesque origin.

MUQARNAS
The soffit of the arches is composed of reduplications of the *muqarnas*, the fundamental element of Islamic decoration. These ornate corbeled brackets form the complex geometric vaulting of the honeycombed domes and arches.

PARADISE GARDEN
The quadripartite arrangement of the courtyard, divided by water channels, is a characteristic representation of the Islamic garden of paradise (see p. 54). The courtyard would originally have been planted with fragrant herbs and flowers.

WATER BASIN
The central water basin is surrounded by 12 stone lions, each fitted with a water spout playing into the circular channel. The spray of water humidifies the dry air and creates the soothing and cooling effect of moving water.

WATERCOURSE
A watercourse is cut into the stone paving, channeling water from the symmetrical pavilions toward the central basin.

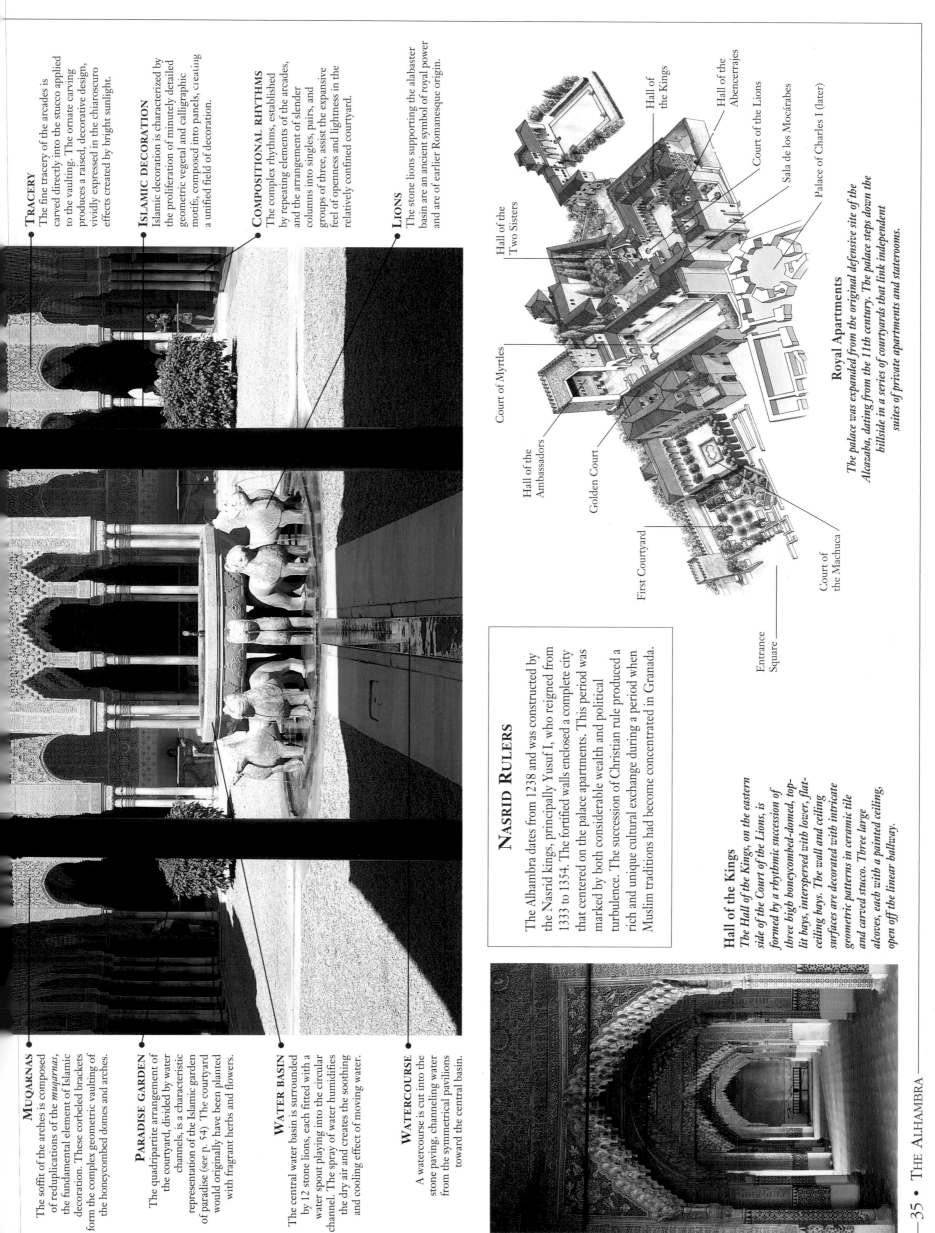

Hall of the Two Sisters

Hall of the Kings

Hall of the Abencerrajes

Court of the Lions

Sala de los Mocárabes

Palace of Charles I (later)

Court of Myrtles

Hall of the Ambassadors

Golden Court

First Courtyard

Court of the Machuca

Entrance Square

Royal Apartments
The palace was expanded from the original defensive site of the Alcazaba, dating from the 11th century. The palace steps down the hillside in a series of courtyards that link independent suites of private apartments and staterooms.

NASRID RULERS
The Alhambra dates from 1238 and was constructed by the Nasrid kings, principally Yusuf I, who reigned from 1333 to 1354. The fortified walls enclosed a complete city that centered on the palace apartments. This period was marked by both considerable wealth and political turbulence. The succession of Christian rule produced a rich and unique cultural exchange during a period when Muslim traditions had become concentrated in Granada.

Hall of the Kings
The Hall of the Kings, on the eastern side of the Court of the Lions, is formed by a rhythmic succession of three high honeycombed-domed, top-lit bays, interspersed with lower, flat-ceiling bays. The wall and ceiling surfaces are decorated with intricate geometric patterns in ceramic tile and carved stucco. Three large alcoves, each with a painted ceiling, open off the linear hallway.

FLORENCE CATHEDRAL

ALSO KNOWN AS **SANTA MARIA DEL FIORE**, Florence Cathedral was begun in 1296 in Gothic style, ornamented with the characteristic inlaid marble paneling of Tuscan Romanesque architecture. Civic rivalry between the ducal states led to the construction of an ambitious dome, raised to a height above the central nave to exceed that of any church in Tuscany. By 1418, the construction of the nave had already predetermined the octagonal arrangement of supporting piers capped by an elevated drum, though the technical means by which to construct the dome had not yet been established. Filippo Brunelleschi's proposal provided a systematic and practical solution, inspired by both the Gothic tradition of stone vaulting and the principles of Roman engineering. The cathedral exemplifies the transition between the Gothic world and the new spirit of scientific and aesthetic inquiry. Indeed, Brunelleschi's achievement set the course of the Italian Renaissance, reasserting Italy's place at the center of a new cultural empire.

Melon-shaped Dome

The melon-shaped dome dominates the Gothic cathedral. Brunelleschi's success in surmounting the technical problems faced during the dome's construction advanced the prestige of Florence among rival city-states of Pisa, Sienna, and Lucca.

BRUNELLESCHI

Filippo Brunelleschi (1377–1446) was the central figure of Renaissance architecture. His studies of Roman buildings gave him an insight into Classical methods of proportion and structure, which he was to apply to pioneering technical achievements and to refinements of composition and proportion.

SPECIFICATION

•**Location**	Florence, Italy
•**Date**	1296–1462
•**Architect of dome**	Filippo Brunelleschi
•**Diameter of octagon**	138 ft (42 m)
•**Building structure**	Brick, stone, and marble
•**Building type**	Cathedral

LANTERN

The lantern was designed by Brunelleschi, but completed after his death. It closes the central oculus of the dome and exerts an additional vertical component of the downward force, reducing the outward thrust at the base.

ELEVATED DOME

The ambitious height of the dome, further elevated by the drum, required a profile that would direct the loads vertically onto the supporting structure. The base of the drum is reinforced with iron cramps.

RIBS

The eight pronounced ribs, 13 feet (4 meters) deep, are supplemented by 16 concealed ribs radiating from the center.

Pointed Dome

Brunelleschi's design, involving a complex structural form and an organized method of construction, reconciled the virtues of a self-supporting dome with the plan of the octagonal, segmental vault. The coffered section of the dome reduces the overall weight of the construction. The herringbone bonding of the brickwork and the concentric rings of masonry blocks pioneered a method of construction that dispensed with the need for centering (a temporary framework) – unmanageable at this height and span.

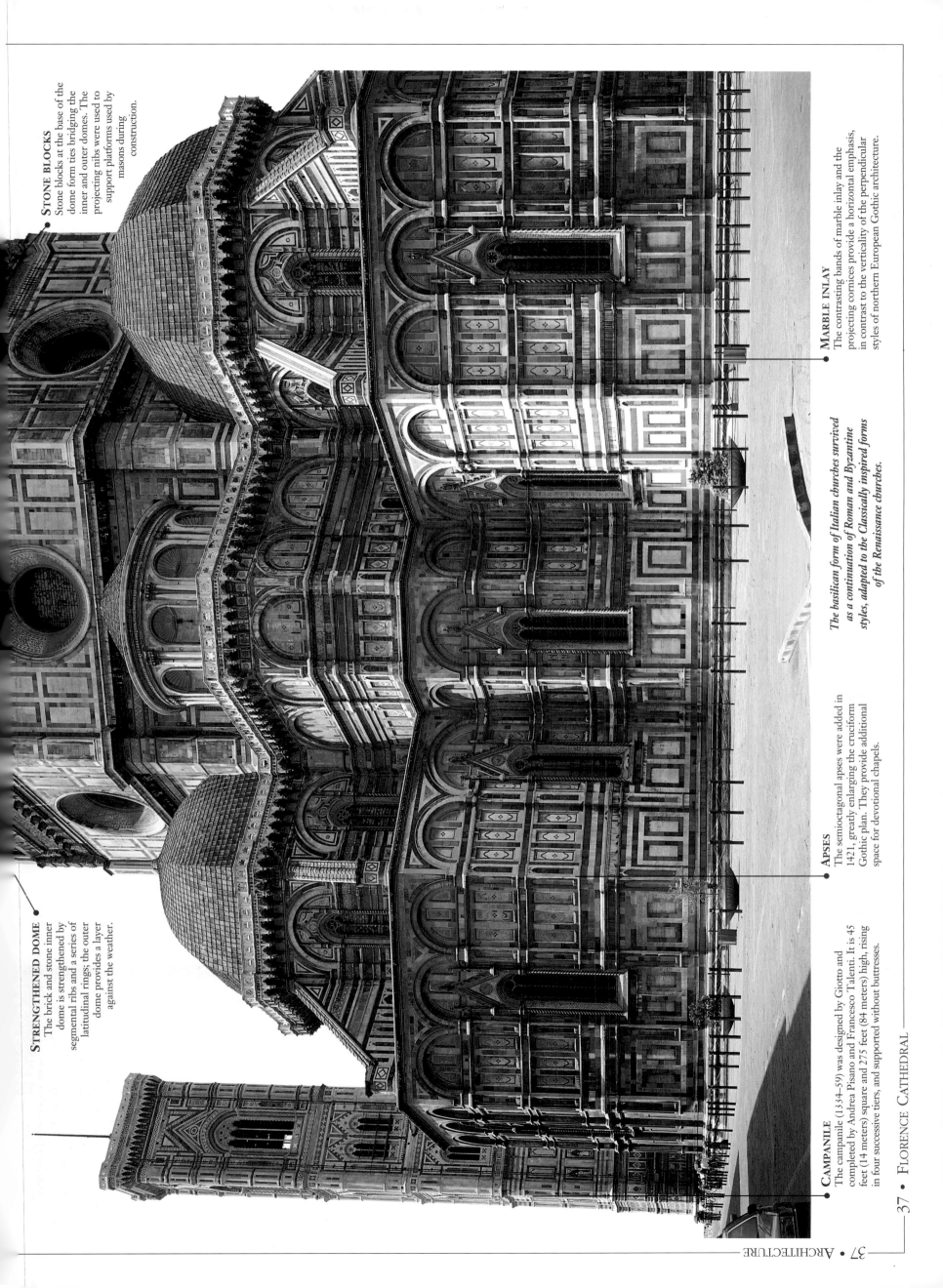

STONE BLOCKS
Stone blocks at the base of the dome form ties bridging the inner and outer domes. The projecting nibs were used to support platforms used by masons during construction.

MARBLE INLAY
The contrasting bands of marble inlay and the projecting cornices provide a horizontal emphasis, in contrast to the verticality of the perpendicular styles of northern European Gothic architecture.

The basilican form of Italian churches survived as a continuation of Roman and Byzantine styles, adapted to the Classically inspired forms of the Renaissance churches.

APSES
The semioctagonal apses were added in 1421, greatly enlarging the cruciform Gothic plan. They provide additional space for devotional chapels.

STRENGTHENED DOME
The brick and stone inner dome is strengthened by segmental ribs and a series of latitudinal rings; the outer dome provides a layer against the weather.

CAMPANILE
The campanile (1334–59) was designed by Giotto and completed by Andrea Pisano and Francesco Talenti. It is 45 feet (14 meters) square and 275 feet (84 meters) high, rising in four successive tiers, and supported without buttresses.

TEMPLE OF HEAVEN

A FUNDAMENTAL PURPOSE OF SACRED ARCHITECTURE is to create a realm that mediates humankind, God, and natural forces. Common to all peoples is a cultural connection between fertility and mortality, and the expression of this connection is linked with the relationship between day and night, the cyclical movement of the sun, and the changing seasons. The calibration of these cycles, through observation of the sun and stars frequently produces a sacred geometry often used as a determining principle in the layout of religious buildings. In Chinese architecture, this extends to the complete harmonization of a building with its site. The entrance and approach are each determined through the ancient art of *feng shui*, with regard to the spiritual influence of environmental features, such as mountains and rivers. The Temple of Heaven in Beijing, China, originating from 1420 (rebuilt 1530 and 1889), is the focus of a ceremony confirming the emperor's temporal power and his authority to intercede with the gods to seek atonement, future providence, and bountiful harvest. The structure of the temple, the raised platform, its relationship with buildings within the sacred precinct, and its position in the city are all holistically predetermined in an attempt to harmonize with divine and natural forces.

The orientation of the temple was established with a magnetic compass, in use since the 8th century, predating its use in navigation. The compasses created for the practice of feng shui have complex scales that are used to interpret the most providential alignment with environmental features and natural forces. They are able to compensate for periodic variations in polar alignment.

ROOF TILES

The blue of the ceramic roof tiles symbolizes openness to the heavens. On construction, the tiles were laid in a strict rotational sequence, with radiating courses corresponding to auspicious numbers.

ENTRANCE

The temple is entered from the south along the carved marble "spirit way," completing the 3-mile (4.8-kilometer) route from the Forbidden City to the sacred altar.

THIRD MING EMPEROR

The emperor Yunglo (1360–1424) was the third and most powerful emperor of the Ming Dynasty (1368–1644). He founded a new seat of imperial power in Beijing and did much to reestablish China following the collapse of the Yuan Dynasty. During his reign, Yunglo led effective campaigns against the Mongols to protect the Great Wall and established his country as a strong maritime nation.

SPECIFICATION

- **Location** — Beijing, China
- **Date** — 1420
- **Height** — 125 ft (38 m)
- **Building structure** — Timber-frame and stone plinth
- **Building type** — Temple

Decorated Frieze

The characters and figures that decorate the frieze and cantilevered timber brackets are of the phoenix and the dragon, invoking a harmonious balance between the forces of yin and yang. The dragon is an auspicious symbol of good fortune, while the phoenix, reborn from its own ashes, symbolizes continuity.

CENTRAL TURRET

The temple's dominating roof structure and platform symbolize heaven, earth, and the passage of the seasons.

The temple precinct contains three structures: the Altar of Heaven, the Hall of Prayer, and the Hall of Abstinence.

TIERS

The three tiers of the podium correspond to the three-tiered roof, as an expression of an odd number with masculine yang associations. The temple is 125 feet (38 meters) high and has an internal diameter of 99 feet (30 meters).

Symbolic Structure

The structural timber frame has three tiers of columns arranged in two concentric rings. The four red columns, 59 feet (18 meters) high, represent the seasons. The 12 outer columns stand for the 12 months, and the 12 gilded, inner columns correspond to the diurnal hourly cycle.

PLATFORM

The temple is raised on a 26-foot- (8-meter-) high three-tiered platform, emphasizing the temple's mediating connection between heaven and earth.

Marble Pavement

The white marble pavement is carved with auspicious symbols and forms the southern approach taken by the emperor when ascending the staircase on a palanquin, a covered litter carried on poles on the shoulders of his courtiers.

KING'S COLLEGE CHAPEL

THE CHAPEL OF KING'S COLLEGE, Cambridge (1446–1515), provides a breathtaking conclusion to the Perpendicular phase of the English Gothic. The simple rectilinear chapel, without tower or transept, was intended as one of a group of collegiate buildings arranged around a central courtyard. The building interior celebrates the fusion of light, structure, and decoration permitted by the evolution of the Gothic vault. The fluidity of the fan vaulting by the master mason John Wastell and the slenderness of the compound piers provide a structural web of astonishing delicacy. Construction proceeded sporadically in three distinct phases (1446–62, 1477–84, and 1508–15), spanning a pivotal phase in European history. As the foundation stones were laid, Brunelleschi's dome for Florence Cathedral (see p. 36) was already under construction. By the chapel's completion in 1515, the political landscape of the medieval world had changed, unsettling the central position of the Roman Catholic Church. While architectural influence was being drawn toward the Renaissance spirit and its emphasis on secular building, England was on the brink of the Dissolution and Protestant reform. The chapel survived the vandalism wreaked on many religious buildings during the period of the Reformation in the 16th century, however, providing an authentic monument to the final phase of English Gothic.

Gothic Arch

The Gothic pointed arch has a greater flexibility of width and height than the semicircular Classical arch. Both are predetermined by the height being equal to the span of the arch. Though the geometry of the pointed arch increases its weight and the amount of material used (the semicircular arch has the optimum circumference), the pointed profile transfers the weight more directly to the ground.

Corner Towers

The corner towers are surmounted by Tudor domes, incorporating the Gothic decoration of crockets and pinnacles. The upper tiers have an open fretwork of quatrefoils and cross quarters to accommodate their use as a belfry, there being no tower as in a conventional church.

CEILING BOSSES

Ceiling bosses relieve the inward structural tension directed toward the center from the radiating fans. This arrangement reduces lateral thrust toward the outer walls due to the low profile of the vault. The bosses are alternately decorated with the Tudor Rose and the Beaufort Portcullis.

COLUMNS

The columns have multiple shafts, which seem to lighten their mass. The structural armature has an amazing fluidity, evaporating within the upper reaches of the vault and providing a perfect metaphorical connection between heaven and earth.

TRACERIED WINDOWS

The upper sections of the traceried windows provide spectacular illumination to the interior. The panels depict scenes from the Old and New Testaments.

The later, and controversial, addition of Rubens's Adoration of the Magi (1634) to the eastern wall beyond the altar completes the perspective view.

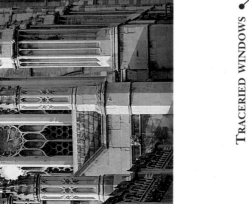

HENRY VI

Henry VI (1421–71) was the only son of Henry V and Catherine of Valois. He was king of England from 1422 to 1461 and 1470 to 1471, having been deposed in 1461 during the Wars of the Roses, a conflict between Yorkist and Lancastrian factions. He founded Eton College (1440–41) and Kings College, Cambridge (1441). Henry VI was murdered in the Tower of London.

CHOIR SCREEN

The timber choir screen, completed in 1536, separates the congregation from the clergy. The medieval framing and Classically inspired decoration and arcade record the transition from the Gothic toward the Classical tendencies of the English Renaissance.

SPECIFICATION

- **Location**   Cambridge, England
- **Date**   1446–1515
- **Master mason**   John Wastell
- **Building structure**   Brick, stone, and timber
- **Building type**   Church
- **Construction time**   69 years

The Gothic vault developed progressively over three centuries. The English preference for decoration was incorporated into the increasingly sinuous and soaring possibilities of the fan vault. The distribution of loads, drawn toward the principal piers through a multiplicity of radiating vault lines, enables a delicacy and lightness of structure.

ROYAL COAT OF ARMS

The royal coat of arms marks the Reformation, a pivotal period in the history of England. The annulment of Henry VIII's marriage to Catherine of Aragon and his marriage to Anne Boleyn precipitated the break with the Catholic Church, beginning a new chapter in English history.

WINDOW NICHES

The window niches, with their pedestals and hoods, were intended to receive statues of the saints. The completion of the chapel saw a change in the emphasis of the liturgy, from the commemoration of the dead to the celebration of the living.

LOWER SCREENS

The lower screens provide access to the side chapels, which run symmetrically along the length of the nave.

Structural Bays

The chapel was constructed in a sequence of 12 equal bays. The uniformity of structure and the buttressing of the wall piers, anchored at each gable end by corner towers, provide an efficient structural frame. The walls between the piers are relegated to non-load-bearing screens, permitting large areas of glass.

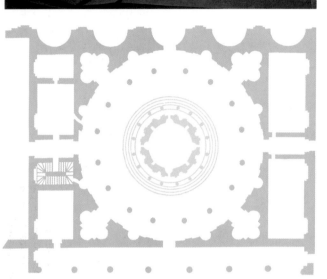

TEMPIETTO SAN PIETRO

THE CENTRAL PLAN held a particular fascination for Renaissance architects, who believed it to have been the prevalent form of the Classical temple and to have symbolic associations with divinity, perfection, and unity. This preference for pure form came into conflict, however, with the requirements of religious worship and the need for the separation of altar, clergy, and laity. The commemorative shrines of the Christian martyrs offered a variation on the functional requirements of the church and a direct Christian equivalent to the pagan model of the Classical temple. The Tempietto memorializes the site of the martyrdom of St. Peter and summarizes, within its modest scale, the striving for harmony and Classical order in the late Renaissance. The central drum, or cella, containing the shrine, is surmounted by a simple dome and is surrounded by a ring of columns, known as a peristyle. The height of the cella is equivalent to the radius, in plan, of the peristyle. The drum is enclosed by 16 Doric columns, in strict proportion according to Classical precedent. The building has a simple unity, based on a system of harmonious proportion with each expressed element related to both one another and the whole.

Plan

The Tempietto is enclosed within the cloister of the monastery of San Pietro on the Janiculum, a hill overlooking Rome. Bramante proposed a complete reworking of the courtyard. Never executed, it would have extended the systematic, geometric proportioning of the Tempietto (center).

Cloister of San Pietro

Confined within the monastery cloister, the Tempietto carefully manipulates the perspective view of the observer to create an illusion of astonishing monumentality for a building of such modest scale, only 15 feet (4.5 meters) in internal diameter. The form, like that of the Classical temples, is best appreciated from predetermined views.

DONATO BRAMANTE

Donato Bramante (1444–1514) was born in Urbino in Italy. He trained as a painter and, from 1477 to 1499, worked in Milan. Under Mantegna's tuition, he developed a passion for Classical antiquity and achieved notoriety for his work on the geometry of perspective drawing. In 1499, Bramante settled in Rome. Under the patronage of Pope Julius II, he gained the commission for the planning of St. Peter's (see p. 44) in Rome.

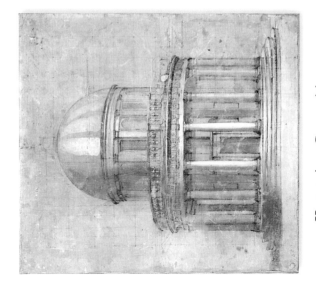

NICHES
Niches within the raised section of the drum derive from the Classical integration of sculpture into the building's decoration.

DOME
Bramante's simple, ribbed dome provided the inspirational form for Michelangelo's dome of St. Peter's, Rome (see p. 44).

Harmonious Composition

Donato Bramante's training as a perspective painter and his careful study of Classical antiquity enabled him to experiment with proportion and order, bringing a new impetus to the High Renaissance. This search for simple, harmonious composition is a departure from the strict replication of Classical elements that was a feature of the early Renaissance.

DECORATION
Bramante decorated the frieze with the themes of the martyrdom of St. Peter and the liturgy of the Christian Church, in a reworking of the heroic pagan images found on Classical temples.

TUSCAN ORDER
The simple and solid Tuscan Order is a slender Roman derivation of the Doric form prevalent in the Classical Greek period.

The monastery of San Pietro was patronized by Ferdinand II (1452–1516) and Isabella of Spain (1451–1504), who are reputed to have commissioned the Tempietto.

COLUMNS
The granite shafts of the columns were retrieved from an antique temple and given a marble base and capital, consistent with the Tuscan Order. Bramante employed a strong Classical Order appropriate to the masculine subject of the shrine.

FRIEZE
The frieze has the Classical Doric form of ornamentation. The triglyphs, panels of three vertical bars, occur at geometric intervals, conforming to the positions of the columns.

SPECIFICATION

- **Location**   Rome, Italy
- **Date**   1502–10
- **Architect**   Donato Bramante
- **Diameter**   15 ft (4.5 m)
- **Building structure**   Stone
- **Building type**   Temple

Bramante was continually experimenting within the limits of Classical proportion and was commissioned in 1506 to work on the exalted scale of St. Peter's Basilica in Rome.

The Tempietto occupies the traditional site of the crucifixion of St. Peter, one of Christ's 12 Apostles. Beneath the building is a crypt marking the position of the hole in the ground created by the cross on which St. Peter was martyred.

CENTRAL DRUM
The internal diameter of the central drum is only 15 feet (4.5 meters). The manipulation of geometric intervals and proportion, together with the practical requirements of size, brings the diminution of Classical Orders to its limit.

ST. PETER'S, ROME

THE REBUILDING OF THE 1,100-YEAR-OLD BASILICAN CHURCH of St. Peter's in Rome (1506–1626) was one of the most ambitious projects of the 16th century. Commissioned by Pope Julius II (1443–1513), it employed some of the greatest architects of the late Renaissance, including Bramante, Raphael, Michelangelo, and Bernini. The lengthy and intermittent progress of its construction illustrates the changing course of the High Renaissance toward a break with strict, antique precedent to the freer, eclectic tendencies of High Baroque and Mannerist styles. St. Peter's reaffirmed the influence of Rome as the spiritual home of Christianity, which had its architectural origin in Bramante's modest Tempietto (see p. 42). Bramante's original proposal (ca. 1506) determined the central importance of the dome and, despite modifications by successive architects, was revisited by Michelangelo's definitive design (ca. 1546) of a centrally planned church, capped by a monumental dome. The cathedral forms the backdrop to the piazza and completes the most memorable formal civic space in Renaissance history.

CROSS
The brass sphere originally mounted at the pinnacle of the obelisk was said to have contained the ashes of Roman emperor Julius Caesar. This was replaced by the cross, into which a relic purporting to be of Christ's true cross was inserted in 1740. Relics are similarly encased in the cross mounted at the top of the dome.

LANTERN
The 87-foot- (26.5-meter-) high lantern is raised 452 feet (137.7 meters) above the piazza, forming a climax to the sculptural Baroque detail of the church. Paired columns reiterate those at the elevated base of the dome and the façade.

Piazza of St. Peter
Looking toward the east from the roof of the cathedral, the elliptical plan of the piazza encircled by Bernini's Doric colonnade makes a grand sweeping gesture, brilliantly illustrating the High Baroque qualities of axiality, movement, and climax.

ELEVATION
With an elevational height of 167 feet (51 meters), St. Peter's is taller than any other Renaissance church, and provides a spectacular backdrop to the piazza.

ORIENTATION
The unusual orientation of the church, with the main façade facing east rather than west, was inherited from the form of the Roman basilican church that it replaced.

Raphael's appointment to the cathedral marks the first recorded use of architectural drawings completed to the same representative scale in plan, section, and elevation. This three-part system became the established method for architectural drawing and survives to this day.

SPECIFICATION

•*Location*	Rome, Italy
•*Date*	1506–1626
•*Main architect*	Michelangelo
•*Height*	452 ft (137.7 m)
•*Building structure*	Stone
•*Building type*	Cathedral

OBELISK
The obelisk, brought to Rome in AD 36 by the Roman emperor Caligula, was moved to its present site in 1586. Raised in complete silence at the pope's orders by 40 teams of horsemen, its re-erection was seen as a triumph for Christianity over Egyptian and Roman paganism.

FAÇADE
The completed façade has a gigantic Order of pilastered Corinthian columns, each 90 feet (27.5 meters) high. The attached columns were modified from Michelangelo's proposal for a freestanding colonnaded portico.

Scale
The scale of the dome is impressive. The pen of St. Luke pictured in the top-right medallion is 7.5 feet (2.3 meters) in length. Around the frieze of the cupola are inscribed the words of Christ's dedication: "Thou art Peter, and upon this rock I will build my church."

STRUCTURE OF DOME
The dome rests on four pendentives and massive piers, each 59 feet (18 meters) thick. Michelangelo's plan increased the strength and size of the load-bearing structure without destroying the central unity of Bramante's original design.

Classical Dome
The ovoid profile of the dome was changed from Michelangelo's hemispheric design because of fears of instability. The construction is strengthened by 16 radial ribs and a double-layer shell (the inner shell preserves the hemispheric form). The dome is banded by 10 iron chains to resist the outward thrust at the perimeter. The structure achieves an internal span of 137 feet (42 meters), only marginally less than that of the Pantheon (see p. 14), but at a much greater height.

BUTTRESSES
The paired columns that buttress the dome were the result of Michelangelo's original intention to build a hemispheric dome.

PORTICO
Later revisions to Michelangelo's proposal for a deeper, open portico produced a design of lesser sculptural impact when set against the monumental façade.

The cathedral is maintained by the **Sampietrini** *– a hereditary corps of workers continually scaling and inspecting the building's vertiginous surfaces. On St. Peter's feast day, they stage a dramatic display by illuminating the profile of the cathedral with thousands of torches.*

MICHELANGELO

The artistic legacy of Michelangelo di Lodovico Buonarroti (1475–1564) dominated the 16th century, bringing a structural and sculptural clarity to the work of the High Renaissance. At the insistence of Pope Paul III, he succeeded as chief architect of St. Peter's in 1546, at the age of 71. Rejecting offers of payment, he undertook the commission "for the love of the saint," and on condition that he would have complete freedom from interference and be without the burden of keeping accounts. St Peter's houses one of his most famous sculptures, *Pietà*.

CRYPT
Directly below the dome and the central altar, in a subterranean crypt, is the tomb of St. Peter, believed to be founder of the Christian Church in Rome.

INCOMPLETE ELEVATION
The later elevation was intended to have been balanced by the addition of two flanking towers. This design was abandoned after fears of instability in the foundations.

COLONNADE
In his original design, Bernini intended to encircle the piazza almost completely, creating an even greater dramatic contrast when entering from the confinement of the surrounding streets.

ST. BASIL'S CATHEDRAL

THE VICTORY OVER THE MONGOL ARMIES at Kazan in 1552 was one of Tsar Ivan IV's earliest campaigns and earned Russia freedom from Tartar rule. St. Basil's Cathedral, overlooking Moscow's Red Square, was built to commemorate this victory. Designed by Russian architects Barma and Posnik, the cathedral established the traditional "tent-and-tower" church as a symbol of national unification and combined the forms of the characteristically helmet-shaped, domed, timber churches of the north with the brick-and-masonry decorative styles of the south. The influence of Renaissance architecture, imported through trading links with Venice, further contributed to this eclecticism. The central "tent" is a separate church dedicated to the Virgin of the Intercession and is surrounded by eight independent chapels, each with its own distinctive tower and onion dome. St. Basil, whose name has become synonymous with the unified cathedral, is buried in an additional northeastern chapel. The fantastically ornate onion domes and profusion of polychromatic tile work are a late-17th-century addition, creating the familiar silhouette associated with Moscow and the Kremlin.

IVAN IV (THE TERRIBLE)

Born in Moscow, Ivan IV (1530–84) was proclaimed grand prince at the age of three, following the death of his father. He was crowned tsar in 1547, and married the first of his six wives in the same year. Although Ivan is known for acts of public brutality, his nickname, derived from the Russian word *grozny*, when properly translated means "awe-inspiring." His reign saw the construction of a centrally administered Russian state and moves toward advancing his country into Europe. Ivan remained on the Russian throne until his death in 1584.

Central church

Octagonal chapel

Chapel of St Basil the Blessed

Polygonal chapel

Plan

The plan is based on a central church with apse, surrounded by four octagonal chapels on the principal axis, interspersed with four polygonal chapels. The simple plan develops into a complex and highly sculptural composition, rising through the triangulated and arcaded drums toward the billowing domes.

SPECIFICATION

- **Location**   Moscow, Russia
- **Date**   1555–60
- **Architects**   Barma, Posnik
- **Building structure**   Stone
- **Building type**   Cathedral

DOMES
The richly decorated domes are a result of later additions to the forms of the chapels. Originally painted white, the church was refurbished in the 17th century to its multicolored form.

CENTRAL CHURCH
The compass points are marked by four chapels with octagonal bases interspersed with four smaller towers on the diagonal axis.

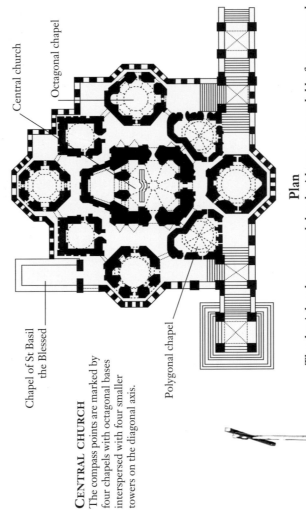

TENT-AND-TOWER CHURCHES
The tiered composition of "tent-and-tower" churches originates from the timber-framed churches of northern Russia.

SYMBOLIC FORM
The central church, surrounded by independent chapels, has a symbolic association with the hierarchy and centralization of Moscow within the emergent Russian state.

Onion Dome
The origins of the use of the onion dome in Christian architecture are unclear, although the influence may stem from the church containing the Holy Sepulchre in Jerusalem. The similarities with Islamic forms are remarkable and betray the Eastern influence of Byzantine architecture.

RUSTICATED COLUMNS
The columns at the corners of each octagonal tower have rusticated stonework, derived from Italian Renaissance sources, illustrating the eclectic use of architectural forms.

CULTURAL MIX
The Romanesque arcade, pointed Gothic arch, and Renaissance motifs are crowned with military crenellations and Islamic domes, producing an exotic blend of Eastern and Western cultures.

BLIND ARCADES
Arranged in ascending tiers, the blind arcades exaggerate the height of the drum, increasing the vertical, stylized tendencies of the domes.

St. Basil's Cathedral is located just outside the walls of Moscow's Kremlin, a fortified citadel containing princely residences, monasteries, and numerous votive churches commemorating tsarist events.

RAISED PODIUM
The brick and tiled church sits on a raised podium accommodating the incline of the site, which slopes from Red Square toward the Moscow River.

VILLA ROTONDA

THE HIGH RENAISSANCE in Italy celebrated artistic endeavor and architectural achievement, with secular architecture enjoying an unprecedented period of patronage in commissions for town houses and rural villas. Antique manuscripts were revived through the new medium of typeset print, popularizing Classical themes. Nature, beauty, and proportion were again studied alongside the poetry of Virgil and Homer, providing an artistic genre for architecture formally set within an "Arcadian landscape." The stylistic excesses of the High Renaissance were to find a perfect foil in the composure and restraint of Andrea Palladio's refined Classicism. The Villa Rotonda (ca. 1552), Vicenza, brings the Classical elements of temple architecture to the service of a civilized place of rural retreat. This image, in its rustic setting, proved capable of indefinite, subtle variation, becoming a model for the understated grandeur of noble houses from the Georgian mansion to the 20th-century Modernist villa, such as the Villa Savoye (see p. 84).

Formal Composition
The Villa Rotonda is situated on the brow of a hill, with the advantage of fine views in all directions. The themes of proportion and symmetry, developed in many of Palladio's villas, are extended to the building's plan and the façade of each elevation. The elemental geometry and strictly formal composition are used to frame both views of the grounds, taken from within the portico, and those of the villa, taken from its landscaped setting.

The rural villa provided a fashionable retreat from the summer heat and the periodic epidemics associated with the increasing density of urban populations.

Architectural Theory
Andrea Palladio's architectural treatise, Quattro libri dell'architettura *(1570), records antique buildings, together with a systematic method of proportion, as well as illustrations of his own designs. This followed a trend established by the revival of the principal surviving 1st-century work on Classical architecture, Vitruvius's* De architectura *(first printed edition, 1486).*

SPECIFICATION

- **Location** — Vicenza, Italy
- **Date** — ca. 1552
- **Architect** — Andrea Palladio
- **Building structure** — Brick and stone
- **Building type** — Villa

Printed editions of architectural works, such as Leon Battista Alberti's De re aedificatoria *(1485), helped to disseminate the influence of Classicism and the Renaissance throughout Europe.*

PIANO NOBILE
The principal living area, or *piano nobile*, is approached by an external flight of stairs, from which a complete view of the surrounding countryside can be enjoyed.

ANDREA PALLADIO

Andrea Palladio (1508–80) reinvigorated the architecture of the late Renaissance with his freshness and simplicity of approach. He completed many commissions for churches and private villas near his home town of Vicenza in Italy, in the studied and reductive Classical style for which he is most famous. Other commissions include the church of the Redentore in Venice. Palladio's influence extended to England and America, where Palladianism became a definitive style of the 18th century.

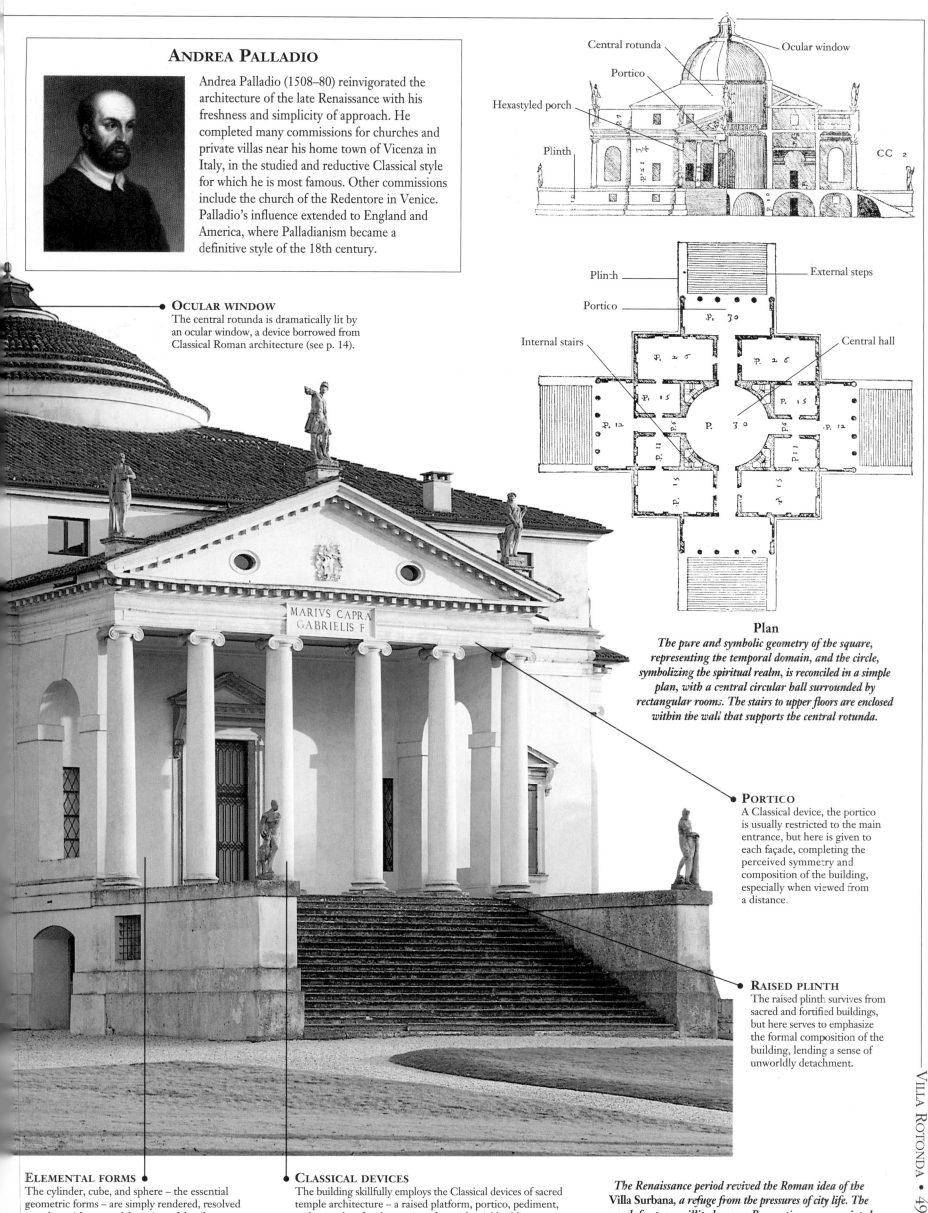

Central rotunda

Ocular window

Portico

Hexastyled porch

Plinth

CC 2

Plinth

Portico

External steps

Internal stairs

Central hall

Plan
The pure and symbolic geometry of the square, representing the temporal domain, and the circle, symbolizing the spiritual realm, is reconciled in a simple plan, with a central circular hall surrounded by rectangular rooms. The stairs to upper floors are enclosed within the wall that supports the central rotunda.

● **OCULAR WINDOW**
The central rotunda is dramatically lit by an ocular window, a device borrowed from Classical Roman architecture (see p. 14).

MARIVS CAPRA
GABRIELIS F

● **PORTICO**
A Classical device, the portico is usually restricted to the main entrance, but here is given to each façade, completing the perceived symmetry and composition of the building, especially when viewed from a distance.

● **RAISED PLINTH**
The raised plinth survives from sacred and fortified buildings, but here serves to emphasize the formal composition of the building, lending a sense of unworldly detachment.

ELEMENTAL FORMS ●
The cylinder, cube, and sphere – the essential geometric forms – are simply rendered, resolved together without an elaboration of detail, to emphasize their volumetric construction.

● **CLASSICAL DEVICES**
The building skillfully employs the Classical devices of sacred temple architecture – a raised platform, portico, pediment, and rotunda – for the service of a residential building, emphasizing the grandeur of both the setting and its occupant.

The Renaissance period revived the Roman idea of the **Villa Surbana**, *a refuge from the pressures of city life. The search for tranquillity began a Romantic genre associated with an idealistic view of nature and the countryside.*

HARDWICK HALL

ENGLISH ARCHITECTURE was slow to acknowledge the influence exerted throughout Europe by the Italian Renaissance. The Reformation had led to a period of cultural detachment, and Queen Elizabeth I refrained from extravagant royal projects, preferring instead to encourage secular building among her courtiers, who vied for her attention and influence. This situation, prompted by the extravagant tours made by the royal entourage, stimulated the personality cult of the queen and a period of conspicuous wealth and construction among the gentry. Hardwick Hall (1590–97) blends the traditions and advancements of Gothic church building (the structural possibilities of glass and stone) with the improvements in domestic comfort demanded by a secular patron. A delight in symmetry and novelty is reflected in its architecture and landscape design. The hall survives in a remarkably original condition, providing an example of the authentic character of English architecture before it came under the influence of the late Renaissance.

High Great Chamber
On the third floor is the principal room of state, the High Great Chamber, used for banquet receptions and musical entertainments. The plaster frieze, including scenes in the Garden of Eden, is a fine example of English decorative art predating the Italian Renaissance influence.

The writer and biographer Edmund Lodge (1756–1839) described Bess of Hardwick as "a woman of masculine understanding and conduct, proud, furious, selfish, and unfeeling. She was a builder, a buyer, a seller of estates, a money lender, a farmer, and a merchant."

COUNTESS OF SHREWSBURY

The Countess of Shrewsbury (1518–1608), also known as Bess of Hardwick, directed her wealth and energies into the construction of the New Hall at Hardwick, which, together with its remarkable collection of original tapestries and furnishings, provides a glimpse of the authentic character of Elizabethan architecture. The house was built following a design by Robert Smythson (1535–1614), who emerged as one of the first English architects to be distinguished from the traditional role of the craftsman-designer. Smythson's designs, also executed at Longleat House (1567–80) and Wollaton Hall (1580–88), show a disciplined, conceptual design, with technical competence and a playful measure of artifice and geometrical invention.

FIRST FLOOR
The extravagant use of glass, which was heavily taxed, was a display of wealth and status. Window openings are supported by concealed stone arches and lintels, which transfer the loads to the walls.

HALL
The two-story-high, centrally placed hall runs from front to back in an unusual arrangement of the plan. This position, rather than the traditional hall running along the length of the building, permits a flexibility of internal planning and a variety of spatial arrangements within the house.

Staircase

The central stairway creates a processional route through the house, which was used for the exercise and amusement of family and guests. The delivery of food from the first-floor kitchen to the third-floor High Great Chamber was undertaken with great ceremony by servants.

Formal Gardens

Delight in symmetry and novelty was continued into the designs of the formal gardens, laid out to complement the appearance of the house. Floral arrangements and mazes of clipped yew hedges provided diversions during exercise taken on the grounds. Gravel paths were laid out among the gardens and orchards.

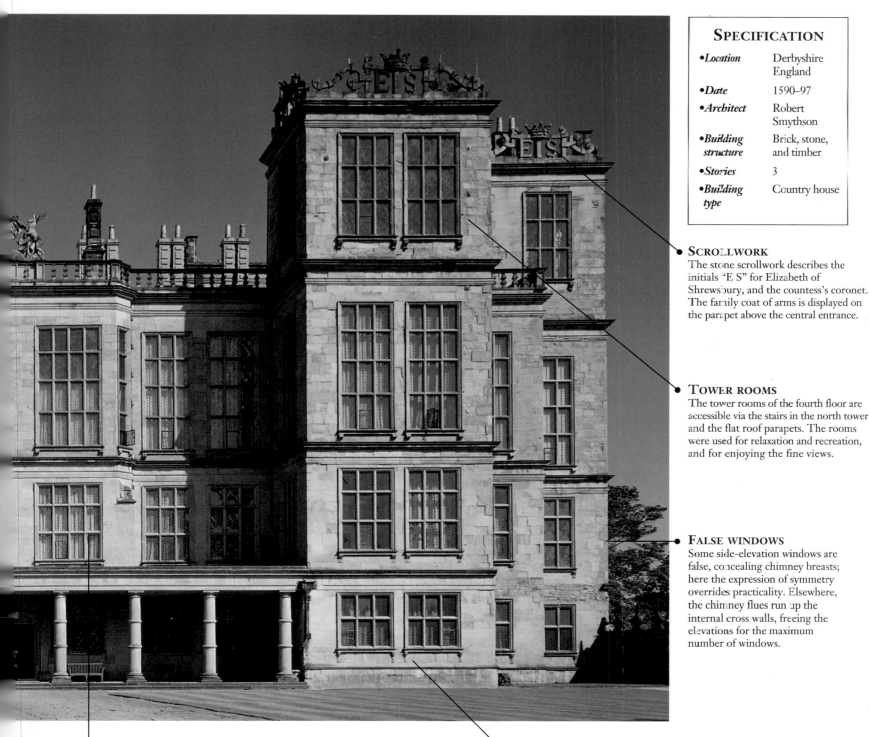

SPECIFICATION	
•*Location*	Derbyshire England
•*Date*	1590–97
•*Architect*	Robert Smythson
•*Building structure*	Brick, stone, and timber
•*Stories*	3
•*Building type*	Country house

SCROLLWORK
The stone scrollwork describes the initials "E S" for Elizabeth of Shrewsbury, and the countess's coronet. The family coat of arms is displayed on the parapet above the central entrance.

TOWER ROOMS
The tower rooms of the fourth floor are accessible via the stairs in the north tower and the flat roof parapets. The rooms were used for relaxation and recreation, and for enjoying the fine views.

FALSE WINDOWS
Some side-elevation windows are false, concealing chimney breasts; here the expression of symmetry overrides practicality. Elsewhere, the chimney flues run up the internal cross walls, freeing the elevations for the maximum number of windows.

SECOND FLOOR
The second floor accommodates an informal dining room, known as the Low Great Chamber; an upper gallery of the chapel; and suites of guest rooms connected across the double-height of the main hall, via a mezzanine gallery, to the private family apartments, bedroom, and maids' room.

SYMMETRICAL FAÇADE
The house is carefully composed on all four elevations, demonstrating the Elizabethan regard for compact symmetry. The rectangular plan is dominated by six towers advanced from the line of the plan. The elevated proportions of the towers provide an imposing arrangement to the façade.

KATSURA PALACE

THE KATSURA PALACE (1620–58) is located near the Katsura River, to the southwest of the imperial city of Kyoto in Japan. The palace and gardens provided a place of seclusion and retreat for a collateral line of the imperial family, in the cultural epoch of the late 16th century. The main palace is an open, timber-framed construction with simple tatami- (rice-straw) matted rooms and elevated verandas from which to contemplate the delicate beauty of the changing seasons. The garden arbors and pavilions surrounding the main palace are approached along a sequence of carefully staged routes, recalling the dreamlike and natural landscapes described in classical Japanese poetry. Throughout these settings, the buildings have an understated simplicity, and the landscape has been subtly manipulated to blur the distinction between artificial and natural environments. Artificial objects, such as fences and paving stones, have been subjected to the forces of nature, such as weathering, while natural features have been clipped, aligned, and polished to emphasize their eccentricity and "unnaturalness." The effect is discreet and alluring, contributing to a heightened aesthetic awareness of the architecture and the landscape.

The buildings and gardens fell into decline in the Meiji period (1868–1912), until "rediscovered" by the Modernist German architect Bruno Taut, who popularized the indigenous forms of traditional Japanese architecture for Westerners. Visitors to Katsura included architects Frank Lloyd Wright, Le Corbusier, and Walter Gropius. They found inspiration in the use of natural materials, simplicity, and a flexible and modulated open plan, suitable for contemporary designs in California and northern Europe.

OVERHANGING EAVES
The low, overhanging eaves allow rainwater to be thrown clear of the building onto the gravel and stone paths that run around the perimeter. The eaves also provide shade from direct sunlight. Soft, diffused light pours into the interior as it is reflected from the stone paths onto the diffusing screens of the paper-covered *shoji* (translucent screens).

PLANTING
Clipped plant displays recede to natural and eccentric forms in the middle distance. The plants create a simple but compelling balance between stillness and movement, between preciseness of form and sheer invention.

THE SHOKINTEI

The Shokintei, or Pine-lute Pavilion, is the most formal of the teahouses. Approached across a bridge of a single stone slab, the path concludes a careful route taken from the main *shoin* (central building). The building has a simple thatched roof and is partially enclosed by rustic screens of timber, paper, and bamboo. A kitchen is provided for the preparation of the tea ceremony, which is performed seated on the tatami of the main room. The pavilion, though raised above the ground, has a more direct connection with the exterior than does the main *shoin*, and the materials are more rusticated. Some of the outer columns are left unfinished, with their bark intact, but all the timbers are carefully burnished and turned to expose their unique and natural characteristics.

TEA CEREMONY

The gardens at Katsura were used to receive guests for the rituals and discourse of the tea ceremony (*cha-no-yu*), which achieved a particular cultural significance in Japan, inspiring works of poetry, calligraphy, philosophy, and ceramics. The aesthetic refinements of the imperial court were, in part, a result of the rise in power of the shogunate, which imposed restrictive codes confining imperial influence to artistic and scholarly pursuits.

Stones
Stones are set in a grass- and moss-covered lawn, providing an informal path to the side of the lake and bridges across to the middle islands and the pavilions. Smooth and jagged boulders are carefully selected and juxtaposed to contrast with the shaped edges and formal lines of the paths, which delineate the building's edge.

The nature of the secluded retreat is typified by the translation of the name of one of the teahouses (Shoi-ken) as the Pavilion of Laughing Thoughts. This was inspired by the poet Li Po, who retired to a hermitage to laugh at the vanity of the world.

SHOIN
The main palace is characterized by the *shoin* style of construction. *Shoin* refers to a place of study, incorporating tatami-matted rooms; a low desk; a *takahoma*, or alcove, for the display of art objects or flower arrangements; and a *chigaidana*, a cabinet for books, papers, and calligraphic materials.

SEASONAL CHANGE
The open form of architecture allows unrestricted cross-ventilation during periods of heat and humidity. The lack of insulation and enclosure is inadequate to protect from the wet and cold of the autumn and winter months. The cultural significance of seasonal change – the anticipation of the cherry blossoms and the beauty of the autumn leaves – is keenly experienced in such a fragile environment.

VERANDA
The bamboo platform of the veranda and the orientation of the elevation provide the best view of the reflection of the moon in the lake. The name "Katsura" has poetic associations with the trees, the moon, and the world of dreams.

THE LAKE
A series of stepping-stones leads down to the lake, which is formed from a natural rivulet diverting water from the Katsura River. The lake was used at night by boating parties to view the rising moon. A pathway encircles the lake, passing each of the miniature landscapes.

SPECIFICATION

•*Location*	Kyoto, Japan
•*Date*	1620–58
•*Building structure*	Timber-frame
•*Stories*	1
•*Building type*	Royal residence
•*Construction time*	38 years

THE TAJ MAHAL

THE TAJ MAHAL (1630–53) is situated on the south side of the River Jumna, near Agra, in northern India. It is a mausoleum built by the Mogul emperor Shah Jahan to commemorate his wife, Mumtaz Mahal. The Islamic traditions of architecture were brought to northern India by the Persian invaders of the 11th and 12th centuries and were continued from the 15th to the 18th centuries in the architecture of the Mogul dynasties. The distinctions between secular and religious buildings are less pronounced in Islamic than in Christian architecture. Islamic practice rejects representative images in favor of abstract design, producing a geometrically disciplined architecture. The Taj Mahal achieves a perfect sense of composition and setting. The building housing the tomb is surrounded by the mosque, hall, and gateway, complementing the overall geometry and composition. The effect is unifying, perfect, and complete.

Marble Dado
A dado (decorative band) runs around the building. The white marble is inlaid with precious stones, amber, coral, jade, and lapis lazuli. In Islamic tradition, flowers are seen as symbols of the divine kingdom.

CALLIGRAPHY
Verses of the Qur'an, the holy book of Islam, are recorded in calligraphic inlays of black stone around the openings.

MATERIALS
The building is constructed from a brick and rubble core, veneered with a fine marble secured by metal dowels.

PRAYER TOWERS
The minarets are placed at the edge of the podium, which elevates the whole structure from the surrounding garden.

REFLECTION
The white marble cladding and water landscaping reflect the changing conditions of light, allowing a subtle range of tones that lend the building an ethereal tranquillity.

Fine Decoration
The recessed, vaulted openings are framed with flower patterns using inlay of semiprecious stones, such as crystal and lapis lazuli, and calligraphic inscriptions in black stone. This detail is continued in the raised relief found in the spandrels and vaults of the interior.

MAIN BUILDING
The main building is situated on the riverbank. The symmetry of this placement, at the edge of the gardens, was to be completed with the construction of a similar mausoleum of black marble, planned on the opposite bank, as the resting place of Shah Jahan.

The pervasive forms of Islamic buildings underline the cultural dominance of the Muslim faith. Islamic architecture is characterized by its reliance on concise geometry and its use of symmetry and balance. Individual design elements are set within a complex, geometric, unifying field of decoration. Architectural planning is informed by the dominant axis of prayer – oriented toward Mecca, Saudi Arabia, the holiest city of Islam.

VISION OF PARADISE
The 17 acres (6.9 hectares) of gardens were designed as a vision of an earthly paradise and would have been extensively planted with exotic flowers and trees.

MARBLE PLATFORM
The mausoleum is placed on a marble platform that raises it above the river's floodplain. A stone embankment protects the gardens from erosion by the river.

FOUNTAINS
The principal axis of the garden is reinforced with water fountains. Water drawn from the river into subterranean chambers was used to feed the canals and irrigate the gardens.

SHAH JAHAN AND MUMTAZ MAHAL

Shah Jahan (1592–1666), the greatest of the Mogul builders, established the city of Shajahanabad (Old Delhi), enlarging the palace-fortress (1639–48) that contains the magnificent Pearl Mosque (1646–54). His legacy is testament to the power, wealth, and energy of the Mogul dynasties. Mumtaz died in childbirth while accompanying the shah on a military campaign.

FINIAL
The central dome is crowned by a brass finial 56 feet (17.1 meters) high.

"Enter thou among my servants and enter thou My Paradise"
THE QUR'AN, SURA 89

The finest masons were recruited to work on the construction. On completion, Jahan is alleged to have ordered the amputation of the chief mason's hand to prevent replication of such exquisite detail.

VAULTED RECESSES
The vaulted recesses lead to the central space, which contains the displayed cenotaphs, enclosed within a perforated marble screen. The actual tombs lie in a subterranean chamber directly below.

COMPOSITION
The minaret prayer towers are used for purely compositional effect, offsetting the central composition of the dome.

Mosque
Pond
Royal tomb
Resthouse
Canal
Great gateway

Plan of the Taj Mahal
The principal axis of the garden runs north–south from the gate to the tomb. The intersecting canals (symbolizing the Four Rivers of Paradise), reinforced with fountains and lined with cypress trees, cross at a raised, central lotus pond of white marble. The surrounding hall, mosque, and gateway complement the overall geometry and composition.

Dome
The main dome, above the central hall, rests on a central drum surrounded by four octagonal towers, each supporting a smaller, domed pavilion. The central, inner dome is 80 feet (24.4 meters) high, surmounted by a raised, outer dome 200 feet (61 meters) high, providing an elongated and slender profile to the outer shell.

SPECIFICATION

• *Location*	Agra, India
• *Date*	1630–53
• *Height*	200 ft (61 m)
• *Building structure*	Marble-clad brick and rubble core
• *Building type*	Mausoleum
• *Construction time*	23 years

WATER
The use of water for humidification, ritual ablution, and cooling is exquisitely exploited, combining religious metaphor with sophisticated devices for climatic control.

CYPRESS TREES
Cypress trees are used to line the stone paths that run alongside the canal. The trees provide shade and accentuate the lines of the perspective.

The purpose of many Islamic buildings is immediately recognizable by their familiar and standardized forms, such as onion domes and minarets.

POTALA PALACE

THE COUNTRY OF TIBET, high on the Himalayan plateau, has long maintained a distinctive cultural identity centered on *Vajrayana*, or Tantric Buddhism, which has been practiced since the 7th century AD. The Potala Palace in Lhasa enshrines the traditions of this unique history in a vast cultural complex that served as a focus of Tibetan politics, religion, and history. The palace is 1,312 feet (400 meters) long and 13 stories high. It incorporates the White Palace (1645–90), which was built by the 5th Dalai Lama to mark the reestablishment of the Tibetan capital, and the Red Palace (1690–94), which was constructed following his death in 1682. Replacing an earlier monastery built in the 7th century, the White Palace housed the functions of state, monastic dormitories, and palace apartments. It encircles the Red Palace, which accommodates reliquaries and holy tombs. The building is a poignant reminder of the suppression of Tibetan culture following the Chinese invasion in 1950, and the subsequent exile of the current 14th Dalai Lama in 1959.

Wheel of Life
The gilded wheel decorating the eaves symbolizes the wheel of life, representing the cyclical nature of life, or rebirth, often used to illustrate Buddhist teaching. The eight spokes represent the eightfold path toward enlightenment.

TOMBS OF THE DALAI LAMAS
The Red Palace contains the shrine rooms, reliquaries, and *chorttens* – tombs containing the richly decorated and embalmed bodies of eight previous Dalai Lamas.

STONE WALLS
The rough stone walls rise 13 stories up the side of the mountain, succeeding to the rendered walls of the upper levels. The red walls are painted annually with pigment by workers lowered down by yak-hair ropes.

WESTERN COMPOUND
The Namgyal monastery, in the western compound, houses the 200 monks who traditionally attend to the palace.

The size of the openings increase in the upper levels, bringing light, views, and ventilation to the imperial apartments. The cell of the Dalai Lama is said to be only 5 x 5 feet (1.5 x 1.5 meters).

SPECIFICATION

- *Location*   Lhasa, Tibet
- *Date*   1645–94
- *Height*   656 ft (200 m)
- *Building structure*   Brick and stone
- *Building type*   Palace

Decoration
The vividly colored and highly ornate forms of decoration, such as these gilded door fittings, are derived from Chinese and Indian influences, imported with the introduction of Buddhism, and mixed with the ancient occult traditions of indigenous art and architecture.

Processional Route
The palace is approached by a succession of gateways and courtyards, used to stage religious festivals. The processional route, with its variety of spatial experiences undertaken by all visitors, pilgrims, petitioners, and state visitors alike, is a metaphorical allusion to the successive paths of spiritual enlightenment.

DALAI LAMA

The Dalai Lama holds the spiritual and temporal authority of the Tibetan people, administered since the 17th century from the palace at Lhasa. Following the incumbent's death, the succeeding Dalai Lama is chosen following a long and far-reaching search by senior monks for the child reincarnation of the Lama's spirit. The child is fostered by monks and brought up in the palace, ruled by a regent and council until the age of accession is reached.

GILDING
The gilded turrets of the shrines and halls are decorated in the Tibetan manner, with symbols representing victory over the world's suffering. The gilding of the Shrine Hall contains 4.25 tons (4.3 tonnes) of gold.

EAST COURTYARD
The vast 172,224-square-foot (16,000-square-meter) east courtyard is used to stage religious festivals held to mark events of the Buddhist calendar.

SILK AWNINGS
The windows are hung with black yak-hair curtains and bright silk awnings. For particular festivals, a gigantic silk banner is unfurled across the steep palace wall.

HIGH PLATFORM
The boundary between the secular and the sacred world of the palace precinct is marked by the high platform.

LOWER FLOORS
The lower floors contain underground storage rooms and are said to conceal the darkened Bon shrines of the pre-Buddhist earth cult.

WALLS
The walls are 1,312 feet (400 meters) wide and 656 feet (200 meters) high. They were built up from the cliff face using stones carried long distances by porters and pack horses.

ST. PAUL'S CATHEDRAL

OLD ST. PAUL'S WAS DESTROYED by the Great Fire of London in 1666. The original scheme for the new cathedral, preferred by the architect Sir Christopher Wren, proposed a centralized Greek cross, without nave or aisles, crowned by an octagonal dome. This design was rejected by the church commission, which was unwilling to depart radically from the elongated, Gothic cruciform plan. The plan was reworked, but the approved design, executed between 1675 and 1710, continued to be developed in accordance with Wren's preference for a Baroque church dominated by an elevated, central rotunda. The cathedral was rebuilt on the same site as Old St. Paul's. The dome, both internally and externally, is its most striking architectural achievement, rivaling those of St. Peter's, Rome (see p. 44), and Florence Cathedral (see p. 36), which it equals in structural innovation. Wren's genius was as both a mathematician and a practical architect, able to resolve all elements – from the general form to particular details – into a fluid and balanced design. St. Paul's brought a stately magnificence to the London skyline and is the central achievement of English Baroque architecture.

The Dome
The dome has a triple-layer construction. The external cupola of timber support bracing and lead sheathing rests on the intermediate brick cone, which also supports the weight of the stone lantern, ball, and cross. This cone is strengthened with iron bands, which reinforce the brick dome. The inner brick dome is fashioned to achieve a lightness of internal decoration.

Ocular windows

Lantern

Supporting timber framework

Brickwork cone

Outer dome

Inner dome

Clerestory windows

Elevated rotunda

CLERESTORY WINDOWS
Clerestory light is transmitted directly into the interior through the elevated windows around the drum, and indirectly through ocular windows at the base of the lantern and the apex of the inner dome.

Wren's confident authority, based on a Classical vocabulary, enabled the design to achieve a harmonious unity that exceeds any formulaic adherence to antique precedent.

ELEVATED DRUM
The prominence of the dome is achieved by an elevated drum, giving the building its characteristic profile.

OUTER DOME
The lead-covered outer dome is supported by a lightweight timber frame, 101 feet (30.8 meters) in diameter. The increased height, raised by the elevated drum, rivals that of the dome of St. Peter's in Rome.

LANTERN
The 850-ton (836-tonne) lantern, supported by the brickwork cone, provides a significant vertical component to the loading, helping to counter the outward thrust of the dome at its base.

CLASSICAL PROFILE
The dome was continually revised in successive designs, developing from a cupola, surmounted by a gothicized spire, into the Classical profile that completes the composition.

Side Elevation
The false windows and increased height of the side elevation screen the buttressing required by the nave walls of the elongated, Gothic plan. Wren carefully considered the many aspects of the building's elevations, measuring them against its overall appearance as a unified design.

TOWERS
The skillful and restrained handling of the towers, as distinguished, individual elements within the overall design, exemplifies the fluidity of the English Baroque.

Structural science was in its infancy in the late 17th century. In 1638, Galileo published his Dialogue Concerning Two New Sciences, which begins to identify a scientific basis for the strength of materials and the resolution of structural forces. Sir Isaac Newton (1642–1727) then provided a significant advancement in his Laws of Motion. Both Wren and Robert Hooke (1635–1703), founders of the Royal Society, studied the theoretical nature of forces.

ST. PAUL
Statues are placed prominently within the façade at elevated positions. The statue of St. Paul, above the central portico, is flanked by statues of St. John (right) and St. Peter (left).

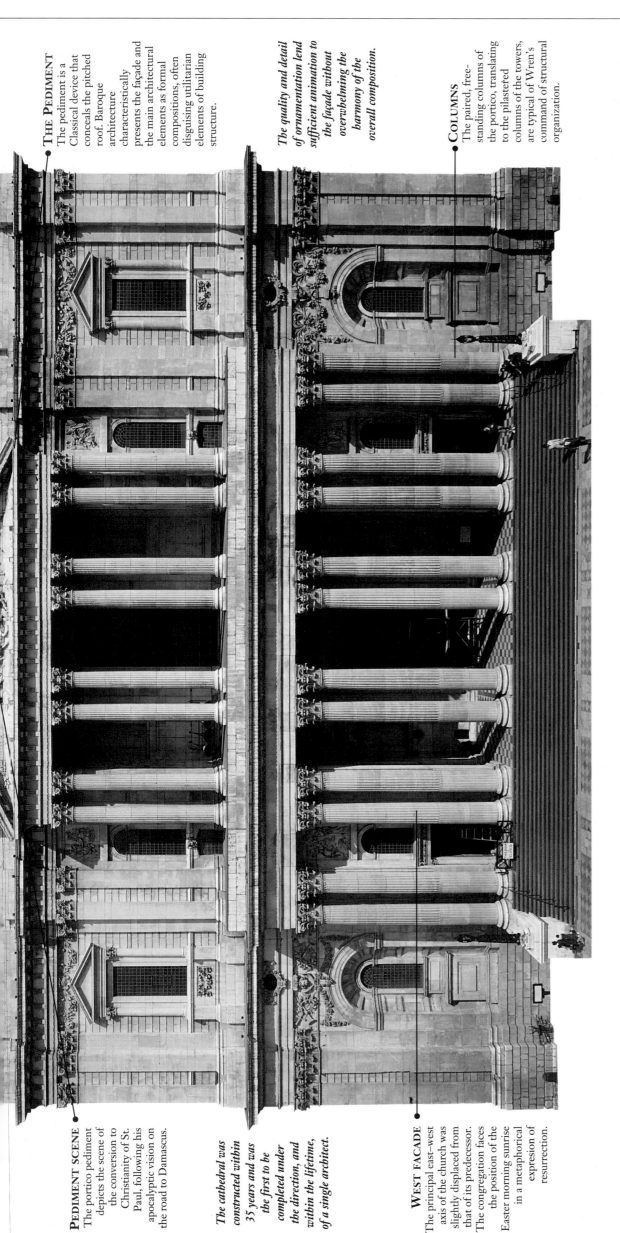

THE PEDIMENT
The pediment is a Classical device that conceals the pitched roof. Baroque architecture characteristically presents the façade and the main architectural elements as formal compositions, often disguising utilitarian elements of building structure.

PEDIMENT SCENE
The portico pediment depicts the scene of the conversion to Christianity of St. Paul, following his apocalyptic vision on the road to Damascus.

The cathedral was constructed within 35 years and was the first to be completed under the direction, and within the lifetime, of a single architect.

The quality and detail of ornamentation lend sufficient animation to the façade without overwhelming the harmony of the overall composition.

COLUMNS
The paired, free-standing columns of the portico, translating to the pilastered columns of the towers, are typical of Wren's command of structural organization.

WEST FAÇADE
The principal east–west axis of the church was slightly displaced from that of its predecessor. The congregation faces the position facing the Easter morning sunrise in a metaphorical expression of resurrection.

SIR CHRISTOPHER WREN

The architectural contribution made by Sir Christopher Wren (1632–1723) in the rebuilding of London after the Great Fire in 1666, and his background in the scientific inquiry of the time, mark him as one of the great minds of his age. Wren was appointed as one of three Royal Commissioners charged with replanning the City of London following the fire. One of his main architectural commissions was the rebuilding of 52 churches in the City of London between 1670 and 1711.

SPECIFICATION

•Location	London, England
•Date	1675–1710
•Architect	Sir Christopher Wren
•Height	366 ft (111.5 m)
•Building structure	Brick and stone
•Building type	Cathedral
•Construction time	35 years

"It seems very unaccountable that the generality of our late architects dwell so much on the ornamental, and so slightly pass over the geometrical, which is the most essential part of architecture"
SIR CHRISTOPHER WREN

Central Crossing

The dome spans the combined width of both nave and aisles, lightening the central crossing and lending grandeur to services and occasions of state. The change from a Greek to a Latin cross required a skillful handling of the plan, to allow the loads from the dome to be transferred to the ground. This was achieved by having the significant weight of the dome and lantern borne by the piers forming the vestries and stairs.

CASTLE HOWARD

By THE LATE 17TH CENTURY, the belated influence of the Italian Renaissance had passed into England through the work of Inigo Jones and Sir Christopher Wren (see p. 58), becoming the definitive style for the cultural aspirations of wealthy patrons. This process of assimilation into the temperate English climate and the context of fashionable society provided ample opportunity for stylistic developments of the English Baroque under the distinctive personalities of its patrons, architects, and craftsmen. Castle Howard (1699–1726), in Yorkshire, England, enabled Sir John Vanbrugh, through the considerable wealth and enthusiasm of his patron, Lord Carlisle, to exploit his bold and remarkable architectural vision, carefully staged amid the dramatic possibilities of its setting. Vanbrugh, in his first major commission, was indebted to the contribution of Wren's former assistant, Nicholas Hawksmoor, whose experience was invaluable to the execution of the scheme. Vanbrugh's facility for grandiose, but lively, formal arrangements, emphasizing mass and monumentality, lends a distinctively theatrical quality to this Baroque composition.

Approach
The house is approached by a formal sequence of crenellated gateways, a pyramid, and an obelisk, arranged purposefully in the landscape. The 5-mile- (8-kilometer-) long formal axis is diverted in the final sequence, bringing the visitor laterally across the north façade, to the entrance court. The formal gardens and fountain are visible from the principal rooms of the south elevation.

SPECIFICATION

- **Location** — Yorkshire, England
- **Date** — 1699–1726
- **Architects** — Sir John Vanbrugh, Nicholas Hawksmoor
- **Building structure** — Stone and timber
- **Building type** — Country house

BAROQUE DEVICES
Vanbrugh's style brings a characteristically bold and monumental handling to the composition. The form of the building employs the familiar Baroque devices of recession and projection. The design is carefully articulated to provide a variety of controlled elements that defer to the overall mass and unity of the composition.

CENTRAL DOME
The central dome appeared as a later amendment to the original design, helping to unify the composition of the broad wings and underline the central importance of the main house.

Vanbrugh's abrupt transition from playwright to architect was lampooned by the writer and clergyman Jonathan Swift: "Vanbrugh's genius without thought or lecture is widely turned to architecture."

CORRIDOR
The connection of the main house with the wings provides an ambulatory corridor, used as a gallery for art and curiosities and for taking sheltered exercise.

EAST WING
Construction began with the east wing, which was followed by the main body of the house. Attention was then directed toward the landscaping of the grounds before completion of the west wing.

SERVICE WINGS
Additions to the service wings required the demolition of the former residence, Henderskelfe Castle, from which Castle Howard derives its name.

STONE
The honey-colored ashlar stone, laid with deeply pronounced coursing lines, was taken from local quarries opened up on the estate.

SIR JOHN VANBRUGH

Sir John Vanbrugh (1664–1726) directed his attention to architecture following a career as a commissioned soldier, spy, and writer of Restoration comedies, such as *The Provok'd Wife* (1697). As a wit and eminent Whig, he was able to exploit his social position. Vanbrugh's introduction to Nicholas Hawksmoor (1661–1736) facilitated his desire to become a grand architect to the aristocracy. His appointment as comptroller at the Office of Works in 1702 and the commission for Blenheim Palace (1705–24) firmly established his reputation and influence within the English Baroque.

THE TEMPLE OF THE FOUR WINDS

Central rotunda

Portico

Elevated base

Symmetrical façade

The Temple of the Four Winds is a miniaturized derivation of Andrea Palladio's Villa Rotonda (see p. 48) and demonstrates Vanbrugh's increasing virtuosity of composition within the confines of a reduced scale. The siting of the temple and Nicholas Hawksmoor's Mausoleum – a derivation of Bramante's Tempietto (see p. 42) – extend the architecture into the landscape, providing a culminating achievement of the English Baroque. The architectural use of such settings anticipates the poignant beauty of the English Picturesque landscape tradition.

Central Hall
Crowned by an elevated dome, the Central Hall has a typically grand and elaborately detailed Baroque interior. The dome was destroyed by fire in 1940 and largely rebuilt. The ceiling, painted by Giovanni Pellegrini in 1709, depicts the story of Phaeton, who drove Apollo's Chariot of the Sun and fell to earth. The scene parodies Lord Carlisle's own political misfortunes and the recent defeat of the French "Sun King," Louis XIV, at the Battle of Blenheim in 1704.

ELEVATION
Vanbrugh's design boldly repositioned the house, with the main entrance elevation facing north and the principal rooms facing south, thus providing the best aspect and prominently displaying the house on the ridge of the hill.

SCALE
The extended reach of the wings exaggerates the impression of the scale of the main house. Vanbrugh's plan maintains a controlled sense of movement within a unified composition.

SCULPTURAL SURFACE
The carving of military insignia, cherubs, and sculptures is the work of the French craftsman Nadauld, whose contribution adds greatly to the fluidity of the façade.

WEST WING
The west wing (1753–59) by Sir Thomas Robinson was completed only after the deaths of Vanbrugh, Hawksmoor, and Lord Carlisle. It is much altered from the proposed scheme and presents inconsistencies in massing and detail with the original building.

PALLADIAN STYLE
The lateral wings connect to the main body of the house. This form, though more compact, is a derivation of the outstretched plans of Palladian rural villas.

GRANDIOSE PLANNING
The planning of the landscape required the displacement of the existing settlement of Henderskelfe, which was rebuilt at a discreet distance from the main house for the estate workers and their families.

Vanbrugh's commission for Castle Howard in 1699 displaced Lord Carlisle's original architect, William Talman. Vanbrugh's commission continued until his death in 1726.

ROYAL PAVILION

THE ROYAL PAVILION (1815–21) in the fashionable English seaside resort of Brighton, described as "a mad house and a house run mad," was used to host the entertainments of the Prince Regent (later George IV) in the closing years of the *ancien régime*. It was transformed from its earlier Palladian style house into a flamboyant palace in the eclectic and whimsical taste of the Picturesque. The oriental style of Mogul Indian architecture used for the exterior and the earlier Chinoiserie of the interior clothe a building that, though thoroughly European in its conception as a royal pleasure house, conveys the Eastern mystical mood of exotic illusion made fashionable in the works of the Romantic poets. The degree of craftsmanship and artifice is astonishing. The architect, John Nash, elaborated on previous schemes by Humphry Repton and James Wyatt, and his designs challenge the boundaries of both good taste and technological achievement of the day. Cast iron, in early structural use, was disguised for the domestic interior as bamboo, and gas lighting was installed to display the interior to its greatest advantage.

JOHN NASH

John Nash (1752–1835) was accomplished in a range of architectural styles. The simple geometry and sweeping curves of his town houses epitomize Regency elegance. Their white stuccoed exteriors with restrained Classical detailing are, however, strangely removed from the fantastic schemes devised for grand private commissions.

SPECIFICATION

- **Location** — Brighton, England
- **Date** — 1815–21
- **Architect** — John Nash
- **Building structure** — Brick, stone, cast iron, and timber
- **Building type** — Royal residence

COMPOSITIONAL UNITY
The smaller domes are included purely for the compositional unity of the silhouette, having no function above the drawing rooms adjoining the main salon.

TURRET STAIRCASE
The Gothic-parapeted, circular staircase in the turret provides access to the upper dome, modified to accommodate three bedrooms, each with windows and fireplaces.

The Pavilion was sold in 1850 by Queen Victoria to Brighton's town council to raise funds for the enlargement of Buckingham Palace in London.

STUCCO FACADES
The façades are faced in stucco, a characteristic feature of Nash's buildings. The domes also were originally rendered and scored with joint lines and colored to simulate Bath stone (a form of limestone).

TRACERY SCREEN
The curved stone arcade is fitted between the freestanding columns of the exterior. The horseshoe lattice, derived from the Indian *Jali* (screen), protects the interior from direct sunlight.

Music Room

The Music Room is the climax of Nash's fantasy. Pendant gaslights in lotus-leaf-shaded glass lamps light the glittering domes, formed by overlapping tiers of gilded scallop shells. The lower frieze is illuminated by back-lit panels of glass. Flying dragons support the silk and tasseled drapery. Gilded balls, bells, and entwined serpents provide encrusted ornamentation bordering the Chinese scenes painted on the wall panels. The organ, when installed, was the loudest in the country.

Iron Frame

A cast-iron framework is superimposed over the main salon, providing the distinctive form of the dome and supporting the Billiard Room in the turret. Elsewhere, cast iron is used as an exposed finish, creating a "bamboo" staircase and "palm-tree" columns. Nash's advanced technology is the first recorded use of cast iron in a domestic interior.

ENVELOPING STRUCTURE
The central dome was constructed from an iron frame superimposed over the main salon, leaving the original interior intact. The enveloping structure was sturdy enough to take an oval-shaped Billiard Room and two other salons.

This exotic fantasy was a fashionable indulgence of the hopelessly extravagant Prince Regent. Nash developed the Picturesque genre throughout the 18th century, represented in a diverse confection of styles, from Oriental to Gothic.

MARQUEE-FORM ROOF
The marquee-form roof of the pagoda dome covering the Banqueting Room and Music Room was the first to appear above the parapet of the existing building, announcing the Oriental flavor of future compositions.

ONION DOME
The central onion dome, derived from Mogul architecture (see p. 54), is a visual metaphor, both exotic and familiar, symbolizing the extended reach of the British Empire.

SCREEN WALL
The bow fronts of the earlier Palladian villa remain, but are disguised by a ground-floor screen wall with doors opening onto the lawn.

Having narrowly escaped demolition, the pavilion has since been used for a variety of purposes, including a hospital for Indian soldiers during World War II.

ALTES MUSEUM

THE GREEK REVIVAL (1790–1830) saw a continuing fascination with the architectural styles of Classical antiquity, encouraged by archaeological finds in Europe and the Middle East. The restrained, elemental style of Karl Friedrich Schinkel sought a new, Romantic expression of Classicism appropriate to the monumental forms of a progressive city. Placed among Berlin's principal civic buildings, the Altes Museum (1824–28) adapts the model of the Greek *stoa* (detached, open colonnade) for the use of a largely 19th-century invention – the art gallery. The museum faces the royal residence across an open square and is approached by a flight of steps, bringing visitors under the Ionic colonnade and through to the central rotunda. The open staircase lobby of the second floor is used to frame a dramatic panorama, completing Schinkel's Romantic vista of the idealized city.

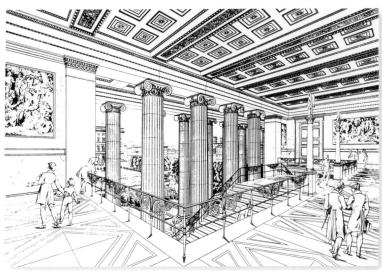

Lobby
The lobby of the main stair, with its double-height colonnade, uses the revelation of a carefully staged vista across the city square to dramatic effect. Schinkel's drawing shows his intention of providing a panorama of the city's monuments; one of the visitors cranes his neck to appreciate this view.

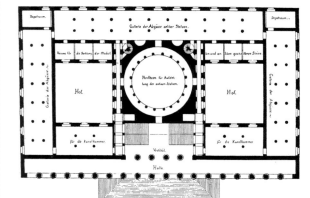

Rectilinear Plan
The rectilinear plan, measuring 282 x 174 feet (86 x 53 meters), is arranged around a central rotunda. Schinkel developed the Enlightenment theories about honest and legible forms of construction; simple, elemental composition; and an expressive use of materials. These ideas challenge the highly ornamented and degenerate style of the preceding Baroque architecture and begin to investigate fundamental attitudes toward decoration and function – issues that became deeply rooted in architecture of the 20th century.

RAISED PARAPET
The dome of the central rotunda is concealed by the raised parapet. The Prussian eagle decorates the entablature.

STATUES
The rooftop statues symbolize the triumph of civilization over barbarity, a grandiose theme that Schinkel saw as an essential purpose of art and architecture.

FRIDERICVS GVILELMVS III STVDIO ANTIQVITATIS OMNIGE

The gallery faces the royal residence and is within sight of Berlin's cathedral and arsenal. The prominence of the art gallery embodies Schinkel's vision of cultural institutions being at the heart of the modern city.

IONIC COLUMNS
The long row of 18 Ionic columns is a 19th-century derivation of the Classical form of the *stoa*, a detached, open colonnade used around the Greek *agora* – the central meeting place of a Greek Classical city.

GRANITE VASE
The monumental vase, fashioned from a single piece of Prussian granite, was inspired by an antique design. Originally intended for the rotunda, it turned out to be too large and had to be relocated in the square.

KARL FRIEDRICH SCHINKEL

Karl Friedrich Schinkel (1781–1841) was an architect, draftsman, and painter who gained an early reputation for theatrical set design in the Romantic style of German idealism. His influence also extended to urban design and landscape architecture. His early architectural designs employ a range of exotic styles, notably Gothic. Following his travels to Italy, Schinkel undertook commissions for the Prussian state in the reductive Neoclassical style for which he is famous. For Schinkel, this meant not simply a slavish reproduction of heroic styles, but an idealistic belief in the instructive and civilizing role of architecture and urban design.

Coffered Dome
The magnificent coffered dome is lit by a central ocular window in a half-scale adaptation of the Roman Pantheon (see p. 14). The rotunda, designed for the display of the statues, provides a central focus. The galleries are arranged enfilade – as a sequence of connected rooms – on two floors around two open courtyards.

"Architectural detailing and design – the art of architecture – must never hide the larger structural forms"
KARL FRIEDRICH SCHINKEL

SPECIFICATION
- **Location**   Berlin, Germany
- **Date**   1824–28
- **Architect**   Karl Friedrich Schinkel
- **Building structure**   Stone
- **Stories**   2
- **Building type**   Art gallery
- **Construction time**   4 years

INSCRIPTION
The Latin inscription on the entablature reads: "Friedrich Wilhelm III founded this museum, for the study of antique objects of every kind and the liberal arts, in 1828."

Neoclassicism became associated with the propaganda imagery of the Nazi party. The reaction against totalitarianism after World War II did much to promote Modernism, which espoused a truly international cause.

IMPOSING STEPS
The imposing flight of steps approaching the elevated base is one-third the width of the façade and is flanked by equestrian statues framing the entrance.

CIVIC SPACE
The siting of the museum as a backdrop to a grandiose civic space underscores Schinkel's interest in the formal role of monumental architecture and urban design.

MURALS
The walls behind the arcade were originally painted with murals (destroyed in 1945) depicting Classical themes – the triumph of Zeus and the development of the arts.

THE HOUSES OF PARLIAMENT

THE OLD PALACE OF WESTMINSTER in London was destroyed by fire on October 16, 1834. The building of the New Palace provided an opportunity for a work of national significance – a building that would encapsulate the contemporary interest in the Gothic as an authentic national style, appropriate for buildings of religious and civic importance. The competition for its design, which stipulated a building of Elizabethan or Gothic character sympathetic to the medieval origins of the parliamentary system, was won by Sir Charles Barry in 1836. Barry enlisted A. W. N. Pugin, whose authority on Gothic architecture and skill as a draftsman were of critical importance in securing the winning entry. Barry's plan incorporated the disparate functions of a complex institution with the preexisting medieval Great Hall. The unified plan, articulated massing, and carefully composed asymmetry are in keeping with the riverside setting and adjacent medieval towers of Westminster Abbey. The building is a monument to the High Victorian taste for propriety, whimsy, and nostalgia.

Exterior Detailing
The building is embellished with intricate ornamentation, arising from the Gothic form and Pugin's instinctive talent for balancing decoration and structure.

"There should be no features about a building which are not necessary for convenience, construction, or propriety. All ornament should consist of enrichment of the essential construction of the building"
AUGUSTUS PUGIN

VICTORIA TOWER
When erected, the Victoria Tower was the world's highest square tower at 336 feet (102 meters). The fireproof construction of stone slabs on brick-and-steel arches is internally supported on cast-iron columns.

The lifting of materials, equipment, and support scaffolding during construction involved numerous technical advances: traveling cranes, climbing scaffolding, and a revolving formwork powered by steam engines and winches.

ROOF VENTS
The roof has cast-iron trusses between the external, load-bearing walls. Cast-iron plates form an external covering to the roof. Smoke and heated air percolated from the underfloor heating through the main chambers and ceilings and escaped through the vents in the roof of the fireproof construction.

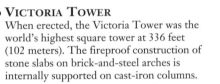

CORNER TURRETS
The polygonal corner turrets, continuous horizontal paneling, and detailing of the parapets were revised during successive stages of the design to emphasize verticality and the skyline.

SUPERSTRUCTURE
The superstructure is of brick and stone load-bearing walls, with cast-iron columns and beams providing internal spans to larger chambers.

BASE
The base rises clear from the water, emphasizing the verticality of the bays. The rhythm of the bays produces what Barry called "tranquillity by the reduplications of similar parts."

FLOORS
The floors are made of brick arches on cast-iron beams, developed from the fireproof construction of industrial buildings. Construction materials were brought by river and stored on the new embankment.

SIR CHARLES BARRY AND A. W. N. PUGIN

Sir Charles Barry (1795–1860) (*left*) was an established architect in the Classical style. His Reform Club (1837) in London is a refined Classical design that incorporates contemporary technology. A. W. N. Pugin (1812–52) (*right*) was a champion of the Gothic style, which he pursued in commissions ranging from pattern design to church architecture. His ideas concerning the appropriate character of buildings and their integration of ornament with structure became influential in the Arts and Crafts Movement at the end of the 19th century.

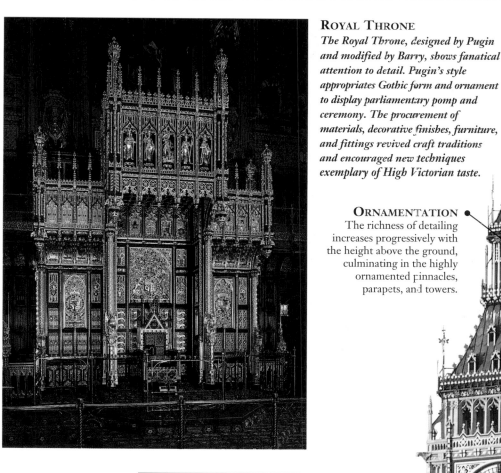

ROYAL THRONE
The Royal Throne, designed by Pugin and modified by Barry, shows fanatical attention to detail. Pugin's style appropriates Gothic form and ornament to display parliamentary pomp and ceremony. The procurement of materials, decorative finishes, furniture, and fittings revived craft traditions and encouraged new techniques exemplary of High Victorian taste.

ORNAMENTATION
The richness of detailing increases progressively with the height above the ground, culminating in the highly ornamented pinnacles, parapets, and towers.

CENTRAL TOWER
The Central Tower, devised by the ventilation engineer, was included contrary to Barry's wishes. The tower ventilates the interior, producing a moving column of air that improves natural circulation.

The choice of limestone and dolomite for the stonework was the result of an investigation into the durability of Gothic construction and its resilience to the effects of coal-burning pollution, particularly destructive in the 19th century.

SPECIFICATION

- **Location** — London, England
- **Date** — 1836–68
- **Architects** — Sir Charles Barry, A. W. N. Pugin
- **Building structure** — Stone and cast iron
- **Building type** — Government building

Clock Tower
The Clock Tower houses the famous Big Ben main chime and four smaller chimes. The main bell was named after Sir Benjamin Hall, the first Commissioner of Works.

FACADE
The three-story façade is 800 feet (244 meters) long. It contains parliamentary offices, libraries, committee rooms, and refreshment rooms, which conceal the debating chambers of the House of Lords (*left*) and the House of Commons (*right*).

EMBANKMENT
The 7-acre (2.8-hectare) site was extended 80–100 feet (24–30 meters) into the river by the construction of an embankment of stone and concrete fill. A cofferdam constructed from a double layer of timber piles and shoring timbers infilled with clay provided storage space and workshops. The water was pumped out, and a retaining wall and terrace for the new building were constructed.

CRYSTAL PALACE

THE IMAGE OF THE CRYSTAL PALACE as the prototypical industrial building in an age of heroic achievement continues to exert its influence within the realm of contemporary architecture. Its history, from its construction in 1851 to its destruction in 1936, provided a premonition of both the beginning and the end of the age of Modernism. The story of its construction illustrates the energy and pace of the Victorian era, whose engineering achievements stand apart from the stylistic arguments that dominated the architecture of the period. Indeed, the realization of the building, without design changes and within budget, owed more to the methods of engineering and industrial manufacture than to the conventional process of architecture. The Crystal Palace was designed as a prefabricated structure for temporary use in London's Hyde Park to house The Great Exhibition of 1851, the first international exposition of industrial design. It achieved remarkable popularity for such a pioneering design and was re-erected, through public subscription, in Sydenham, England, where it stood until destroyed by fire in 1936.

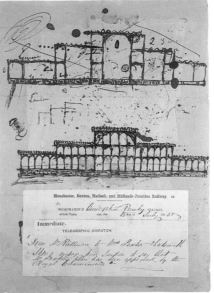

The First Sketch
Architect Sir Joseph Paxton's involvement with the project began with this sketch, which he prepared after hearing that the Exhibition Committee was unable to agree on a winning design from the 233 official entries to the competition of April 1850. Paxton made his sketch after visiting the site on June 11, 1850. By June 24, he had prepared drawings for tender by Fox Henderson and Co. The design was approved by the committee on July 26, and work commenced on July 30. Construction itself started on September 26, and the building was ready for occupation on February 1, 1851.

The Paxton gutter was formed by 24-foot- (7.3-meter-) lengths of machine-profiled timber, made into a bowstring truss, with cast-iron brackets and a wrought-iron cord. This supported the roof and formed a gutter that directed rainwater toward the main structural columns, which acted as drainpipes.

STEEL LOUVERS
Horizontal bands of mechanically operated steel louvers allowed the controlled circulation of air. The glass roof was covered by retractable canvas awnings, sprayed with cool water in hot weather.

GLAZING
Unprecedentedly large sheets of glass, over 4 feet (1.2 meters) long and 10 inches (25 centimeters) wide, were used to glaze the roof and upper sections of the walls.

SPECIFICATION

- **Location**   London, England
- **Date**   1850–51
- **Architect**   Sir Jospeh Paxton
- **Building structure**   Cast and wrought iron, and timber
- **Building type**   Exhibition hall
- **Construction time**   6 months

TABLE AND CLOTH
Paxton used the analogy of a table covered by a cloth to explain the internal frame of cast-iron columns and cast- and wrought-iron trusses that provided a rigid "table" over which an external lightweight "cloth" of glass was draped, framed by timber glazing bars.

BARREL VAULT
The timber barrel vault ran the full width of the central transept; its height enabled the retention of elm trees on the Hyde Park site. Further vaults (seen here) were added to the reconstructed building in Sydenham.

The original construction contract was awarded to the contractor on a "recyclable" basis: the budget was £150,000 for the whole building, or £80,000 if ownership reverted to the contractor after the building was dismantled.

FRAMING MEMBERS
The cast-iron, wrought-iron, and timber framing members were assembled from standardized components. Columns, at 24-foot- (7.3-meter-) intervals, ran the full length of the building.

Rapid expansion of the rail system facilitated the transport of components and materials, enabling collaboration between manufacturers for design and construction, and making possible a quick completion.

The idea of a construction kit of parts brilliantly exploited the potential of industrial production. The advantages of mass production, prefabrication, and systematic site assembly were newly available to Victorian engineers and designers.

The Palace of Industry for All Nations
Prince Albert, husband of Queen Victoria, championed the Great Exhibition, which he heralded as "a true test and living picture of the point of development at which the whole world of mankind has arrived." The exposition provided an encyclopedic array of industrial and cultural artifacts. Over 6 million visits (by nearly one in five of the population) were made to the site during the first five months.

Internal Framework
Internally, the framework was painted in colors coordinating the structural trusses. The slender internal structural frame, cloaked with an external envelope of framed glass, provided an economical enclosure that admitted the maximum amount of natural light.

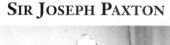

SIR JOSEPH PAXTON

As head gardener to the Duke of Devonshire at the age of 23, Joseph Paxton (1803–65) landscaped Chatsworth House in Derbyshire, England. He developed the construction system for the Palm House that served as a prototype for the design of the Crystal Palace. Paxton was also involved in the development of many rail projects.

DECORATION
Decorative elements were used simply to embellish the hall and to regularize its appearance. The arches, circular openings, pinnacles, and trellis around the roof emphasized the rhythm of the structural bays.

TURBINE BUILDING, MENIER FACTORY

THE **INDUSTRIAL TECHNIQUES** pioneered in the 19th century responded to a proliferation of new building types that were to influence 20th-century architecture. The early use of iron was confined largely to industrial buildings and engineering structures. In architectural applications, the structural frame was generally disguised with an overcoat of conventional architectural appearance. The Turbine Building (1871–72), at Noisiel-sur-Marne, near Paris, supplied mechanical power to the Menier chocolate firm. Its architect, Jules Saulnier, chose to express the skeleton frame, interpreting the mill building as a bridge spanning masonry piers set into the riverbed. The lightweight, wrought-iron frame and thin skin of brickwork illustrate the Rationalist integration of structure, function, and decoration championed by the architect and critic, Eugène Viollet-le-Duc. With its iron superstructure and thin-walled cladding, the building heralded the arrival of techniques that were to revolutionize 20th-century architecture. Decoratively and technically ostentatious, it is a wonderful reminder of the enterprise of the 19th century.

Decorated Surfaces
Nineteenth-century Rationalism sought to integrate structure and ornament with particular relevance to contemporary buildings and industrial materials. Here, the colored brickwork and ornate moldings are responsive to the structural form of the building. Identified as the principle of Gothic architecture, this was to develop into a defining principle of Modernism.

SLENDER STRUCTURE
The building has a sheer face, without recession or projection, creating a slenderness and vertical alignment of structure.

DECORATION
The polychromatic brickwork enlivens the façade and accentuates the geometry of the structural frame. The circular panels are inset with alternating designs of the cacao tree and the Menier monograph.

CLADDING
The hollow brickwork provides a lightweight panel, filling in the diagonally braced wrought-iron lattice frame.

Curtain Wall
The brick wall makes no contribution to the building structure. This had a particular significance for the future of multistory buildings, whose height would preclude the load-bearing support of the external wall. The wall becomes a curtain hung or held outside the frame. This device was to become a leitmotiv of the Modern Movement.

STRUCTURAL USE OF IRON

Cast iron, though immensely strong in compression, is brittle and weak in tension. Exploiting its compressive strength, the first cast-iron bridge was erected over the Severn River in Coalbrookdale, England, in 1779. The "puddling" process, patented in 1784, however, introduced wrought iron, which has greater tensile strength than cast iron, although its use was eventually overtaken by that of steel in 1855.

Lightweight Structure
The mill straddles the Marne River, using the water to drive the turbines to supply the power for the process of refining the chocolate. Braced by the diagonal struts, the whole wall acts as a gigantic lattice truss, producing an efficient and lightweight structure. To clear the main production space of columns, the upper floor is suspended from the roof trusses.

• WINDOWS
The skeleton frame allows an increase in the area available for windows and other openings. Industrial processes, before the advent of cheap and safe artificial light, were often reliant on high levels of daylight.

SPECIFICATION

• **Location**	Noisiel-sur-Marne, France
• **Date**	1871–72
• **Architect**	Jules Saulnier
• **Building structure**	Wrought-iron frame and stone piers
• **Building type**	Factory

• EXPOSED FRAMEWORK
The mill structure has an exposed framework, which was probably inspired by the half-timbered framing of the preexisting mill that Saulnier's building replaced.

• FLOORS
Internally, the floors are constructed from shallow brick vaults spanning onto I-section wrought-iron joints running between the external walls. The third floor uses joists made into a box-section to take the extra weight of machinery.

• BOX BEAM
The hollow-steel box beam, fabricated from wrought-iron plates and angles, spans the stone piers. It forms a composite support with the diagonal struts of the lattice frame.

SAGRADA FAMILIA

THE EXALTED SCALE AND FANTASTICAL IMAGERY of the Expiatory Church of the Holy Family (Sagrada Familia) in Barcelona, Spain, are the vision of the architect Antonio Gaudí, who directed the project from 1884 until his death in 1926. Gaudí's unique architectural style was fueled by a deeply held religious conviction. The Sagrada Familia celebrates the Holy Family and the mysteries of the Catholic faith. The fluid manipulation of stone and concrete is achieved by a complex geometry of vaulted structures surrounded by the campanile towers of the main façades, which become increasingly fantastic, rising up to the polychromatic ceramic surfaces of the "pompom" pinnacles representing the Apostles. Though only partially completed, the building rivals in ambition and scale the cathedrals of medieval Europe. The continuation of the work during periods of political and social change symbolizes the vitality of Catalan culture.

SPECIFICATION

- **Location** — Barcelona, Spain
- **Date** — 1884–present
- **Architect** — Antonio Gaudí
- **Height on completion** — 180 m (591 ft)
- **Building structure** — Stone and concrete
- **Building type** — Church

Wire Models
Gaudí used models made from wire and plaster-soaked canvas sheets, suspended with weights, to represent forms. When dry, they were analyzed for points of weakness, which could then be reinforced.

ANTONIO GAUDI

Antonio Gaudí (1852–1926) was born in Reus, Catalonia. He was inspired by the reawakening of interest in medieval craft guilds among adherents of the Arts and Crafts Movement, and became associated with the Catalan *Modernista* movement. Gaudí developed his career notably through commissions from his patron, the textile manufacturer Don Basilio Güell, such as the Palacio Güell, Barcelona (1886–89), and Parque Güell, Barcelona (1900–14).

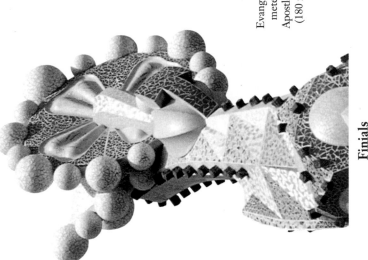

Gaudí had an intuitive genius for structural form, influenced by his knowledge of Gothic architecture and traditional Catalan structures of brick, stone, and ceramic tile.

FLUID FORMS
The highly fluid forms are mathematically generated and subject to a rational means of analysis. This is needed to generate the geometry and undertake the construction – often by means of only simple drawings.

CAMPANILE TOWERS
Four towers represent the Evangelists, and 12 328-foot (100-meter) campaniles symbolize the Apostles. A central tower 591 feet (180 meters) high is to complete the final composition.

Finials
The highly animated surface of the façade leads to the color and decoration of the upper campaniles, inset with ceramic tiles and figures. This detail of the "pompom" finials of the western transept is symbolic of the bishop's miter, ring, and staff.

After Gaudí's death in 1926, the project continued under the direction of his associates. The destruction of the design models and many of the original drawings during the Spanish Civil War (1936–39) halted the construction. By working from retrieved models, architects resumed the project in 1954. The construction continues with fierce debate about the nature of the executed design.

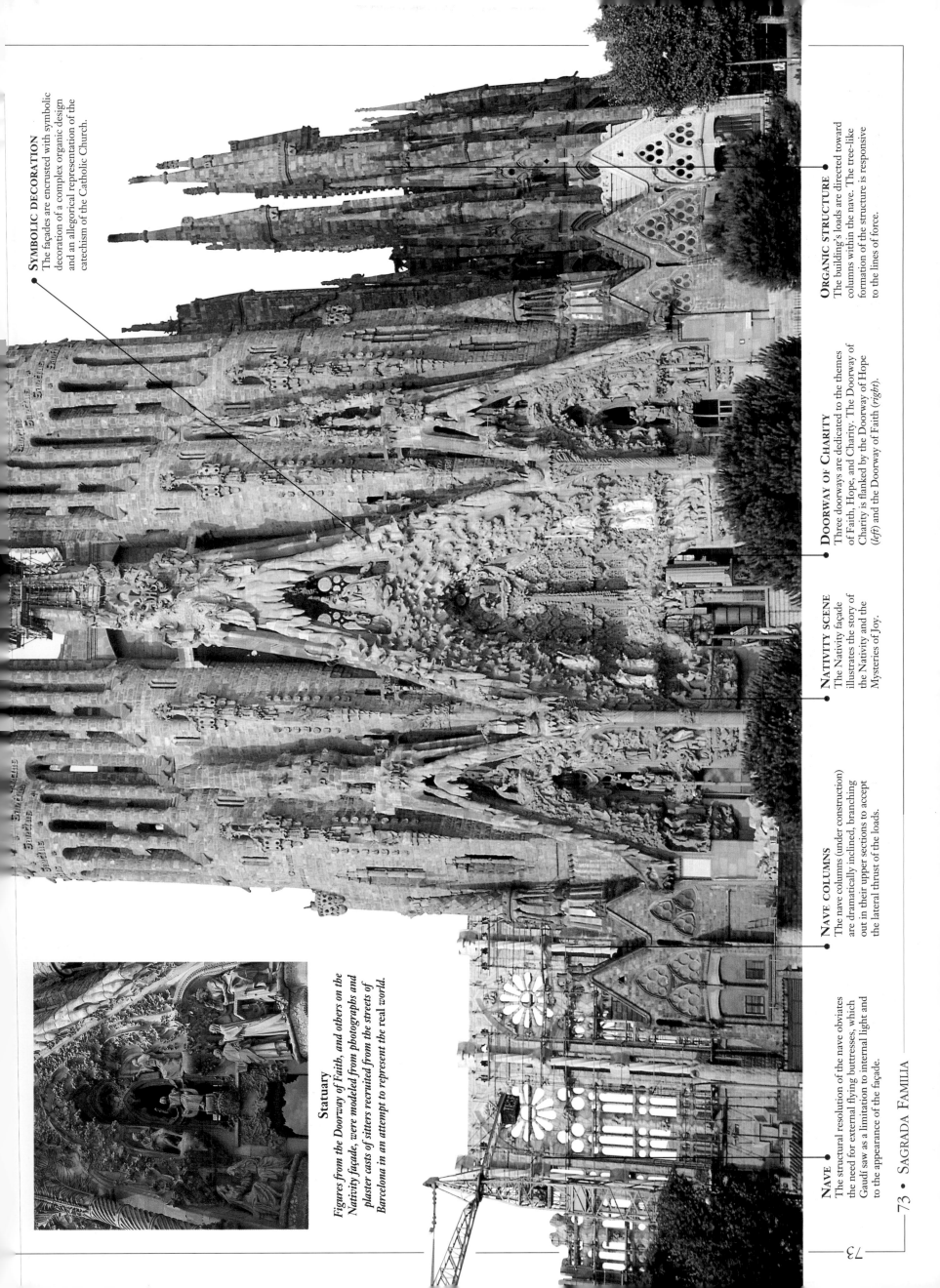

SYMBOLIC DECORATION
The façades are encrusted with symbolic decoration of a complex organic design and an allegorical representation of the catechism of the Catholic Church.

ORGANIC STRUCTURE
The building's loads are directed toward columns within the nave. The tree-like formation of the structure is responsive to the lines of force.

DOORWAY OF CHARITY
Three doorways are dedicated to the themes of Faith, Hope, and Charity. The Doorway of Charity is flanked by the Doorway of Hope (*left*) and the Doorway of Faith (*right*).

NATIVITY SCENE
The Nativity façade illustrates the story of the Nativity and the Mysteries of Joy.

NAVE COLUMNS
The nave columns (under construction) are dramatically inclined, branching out in their upper sections to accept the lateral thrust of the loads.

NAVE
The structural resolution of the nave obviates the need for external flying buttresses, which Gaudí saw as a limitation to internal light and to the appearance of the façade.

Statuary
Figures from the Doorway of Faith, and others on the Nativity façade, were modeled from photographs and plaster casts of sitters recruited from the streets of Barcelona in an attempt to represent the real world.

GLASGOW SCHOOL OF ART

THE COMPETITION-WINNING ENTRY by Charles Rennie Mackintosh for the new Glasgow School of Art (1897–1909) produced a work of outstanding originality. Mackintosh's highly personal architectural style blended paradoxical elements of the 19th-century Arts and Crafts Movement and the European avant-garde with a freshness of approach. His ability to integrate a modern design into a historic setting, along with the building's dramatic tension – between existing sensuality and restraint, enrichment and reduction – established Mackintosh's reputation in a work of enduring achievement. Mackintosh submitted designs under the competition rules in 1895 and was appointed as winning entrant for the firm of Honeyman, Keppie, and Mackintosh in January 1897. Limited funds required the competitors to identify two phases of construction.

The first phase (1897–99) terminated at the main entrance tower of the north elevation, and the interval between phases allowed Mackintosh a period of design revision. The west-wing (1907–9), with its soaring elevation and magnificent two-story library, shows Mackintosh as a mature and confident designer.

ELEVATION
TO DALHOUSE STREET

THE GLASGOW SCHOOL OF ART

4 BATHWOOD ROAD
GLASGOW MORRIS (BG2)

ELEVATION
TO SCOTT STREET

West and East Elevations

The west elevation (left) combines a powerful formal arrangement with the casual asymmetry of traditional vernacular architecture. The surface of the elevation is skilfully composed, the exploitation of the play of mass against void used as an articulation of internal function. The modeling of the towers and bays of the east elevation (right) is reminiscent of the baronial houses of Scottish architecture.

SPECIFICATION

- **Location** Glasgow, Scotland
- **Dates** 1897–99 (Phase 1) 1907–9 (Phase 2)
- **Architect** Charles Rennie Mackintosh
- **Building structure** Stone, wrought iron, and steel
- **Building type** Art school

NICHES

The niches in the wall surface were designed to accommodate sculptures depicting the arts. The stone drums were intended for subsequent sculptural decoration, though this omission emphasizes the simple and powerful massing of the façade.

PROJECTING BAYS

The projecting bays rise uninterrupted through three stories, emphasizing the height of the west wing and the internal volume of the two-story library.

END WINDOWS

The two end windows are one pane narrower than the windows in the other studios. The asymmetry throughout the building provides subtle irregularities of composition that allude to the variations found in vernacular buildings.

North Façade

The building has an E-shaped plan, with main studio spaces arranged along the long north façade. Further teaching spaces and offices are provided in the east wing, with a lecture hall, library, and studio spaces along the west façade.

EAVES

The oversailing eaves protect the studio spaces from direct sunlight and establish a strong profile to the roofline.

STUDIO WINDOWS

The large window areas allow ample natural light to flood the teaching studios. Their appearance in the stone façade evokes both the Elizabethan manor house (see p. 50) and the glass wall emblematic of the Modern Movement.

TINY WINDOW
The tiny window that lets light into the life-drawing room accentuates the thickness and mass of the wall.

CONTRASTED STONE
The rough stone of the studio end walls is contrasted with the dressed course stone around the windows. The junction is subtly demarcated by a horizontal stepped line.

WEST DOORWAY
The fine detail of the door frame relieves the monumentality of the elevation. The doorway has a stepped molding, which anticipates the motifs of Art Deco.

BRACKETS
The wrought-iron brackets strengthen the slender window mullions and provide support for a window-cleaning platform. The decorative finials recall Celtic motifs and are subtly varied with floral designs.

RAILINGS
The railings carry posts with heraldic Celtic-, and Japanese-inspired motifs.

NATURAL LIGHT
The façade is set back from the street to admit natural light into the basement.

The main building is 245 feet (75 meters) long and 93 feet (28 meters) deep. The building has five stories, with an attic story of studios added in the second phase. The site falls 34 feet (10 meters) toward the south, a fact dramatically emphasized by the verticality of composition on the west elevation.

FAÇADE
The treatment of the façade is expressive of the internal function and spatial hierarchies within the building, which is a characteristic of the Modern Movement.

Library

The two-story library has a mezzanine floor suspended from the floor above. This reduces the need for timber framing and emphasizes the lightness of structure. The rails of the dark-stained oak balustrades are discreetly notched and decorated with flashes of primary color. The lights, furniture, and sensitivity of fine detail create a comprehensive architectural interior conducive to the requirements of quiet and contemplative study.

CHARLES RENNIE MACKINTOSH

Charles Rennie Mackintosh (1868–1928) exhibited as a member of the Glasgow Four, whose reputation for decorative arts and furniture, in a severe yet lyrical style, earned them the nickname "Spook School." He built extensively in Glasgow and received acclaim in Europe, but long periods of exile and the intervening years of World War 1 limited his architectural output. A posthumous revival of his reputation by succeeding generations established him as one of the greatest early-20th-century European architects.

Glass Panel
The colored-glass panel on the first-floor door shows the characteristic Mackintosh decorative elements: a Tree of Life, emerging as a woman's face with a centrally placed rosebud. The motifs are stylized, sexual, and symbolic, combining the many complex aspects of Mackintosh's personality.

GAMBLE HOUSE

THE ENGLISH ARTS AND CRAFTS MOVEMENT, with its emphasis on dignity in labor and respect for nature, was introduced to America partly through the religious and utopian communities of the mid-19th century. A crafted use of natural materials and a feeling of closeness to nature prevailed along with nostalgic pride for the pioneering spirit and middle-class American values of the late-19th-century suburbs. The California climate was conducive to this sense of openness, and the traditional form of timber construction was adaptable and accommodating to the rustic image: long, low verandas; sheltering eaves; a centralized hearth; and a direct connection with the garden. Open porches, from which to enjoy the scented evenings, extend the interior. American architect Frank Lloyd Wright had already popularized the indigenous Shingle Style and imported influences of Japanese *shoin* architecture. In the Gamble House (1908–9), the Greene brothers blended this imagery with the climate, finding a delight in the richness of detail and providing a definitive image of affluence and propriety appropriate to the early 20th century.

GREENE AND GREENE

Henry Greene (1870–1954) (*left*) and Charles Sumner Greene (1868–1957) (*right*) studied at the Massachusetts Institute of Technology in Cambridge. They were acquainted with the work of the Arts and Crafts Movement through a magazine called *The Craftsman*, which featured the work of many of the English Arts and Crafts studios. But it is perhaps their affinity with Japanese joinery and traditional *shoin*-style architecture that informs the sensitivity to materials and details that distinguishes the Greenes' work. Other examples of their work are the Blacker House (1907), Pasadena, California, and the Pratt House (1909), Ojai, California.

ARTS AND CRAFTS

Inspired by the socialist utopian William Morris (1834–96) and the architectural writer John Ruskin (1819–1900), the Arts and Crafts Movement of the late 19th century was a response to the deterioration in the quality and design of many machine-made products. It promoted traditional crafts and vernacular building practices and sought to reintroduce the direct relationship between the designer and the maker, exploiting the experience of the artisan and emphasizing the innate characteristics of materials.

OVERSAILING EAVES
The veranda and porches are both shaded and protected by oversailing eaves. The ends of the rafters are exposed, emphasizing the simple arrangement of structure inspired by vernacular forms and Japanese joinery.

TIMBER FRAME
The lightness of construction and inherent flexibility of timber-framed buildings make them ideally suited to areas at risk of earth tremors, such as Japan and California.

SLEEPING PLATFORMS
Balconies lead directly from the bedrooms, allowing the occupants to sleep in the open air on summer evenings. The Greenes' father was a respiratory physician who believed in the health-giving virtues of fresh air and cross-ventilation.

CLADDING
The timber frame is clad with redwood *shakes* – large timber tiles with a natural irregularity and pronounced grain – imparting a gentle, weathered finish to the building.

Hallway

The hallway provides a central core for circulation between levels and areas distinct in the floor plan. The richness of materials and attention to detail here are continued throughout the house. Teak-framed entrance doors, with colored-glass panels depicting the outspread arms of an oak tree, wash the interior with light that is then reflected in the hand-polished timber surfaces.

Staircase

The Burmese teak staircase rises from the hallway. The ends of the beams are rounded, and the screwed joints are capped with distinctive dowelled timber heads. The polished finish emphasizes the color and grain of the timber. The attention to detail and honesty of expression toward materials and construction are characteristic of the Arts and Crafts Movement.

STRUCTURAL FRAME

Traditional Japanese houses use a primary structural frame of large timbers held by complex joints. American frames could be assembled quickly using a larger number of smaller timbers fixed with nails and screws. The Gamble House uses both principles, expressing, where possible, a simple frame, but using contemporary methods elsewhere.

HORIZONTALITY

The line of the roof provides a low profile for the building. The informal, horizontal composition has a softness that blends with the landscape.

SPECIFICATION

- **Location** — Pasadena, California
- **Date** — 1908–9
- **Architects** — C. S. Greene, H. M. Greene
- **Building structure** — Timber-frame
- **Stories** — 3
- **Building type** — House
- **Construction time** — 1 year

PLINTH

The building is placed on a small terraced plinth, which blurs the edges of the building and provides a subtle transition to the garden.

STRUCTURAL EXPRESSION

The redwood frame emerges on the outside and is similarly exposed within. The simple legibility of the building is prompted by the search for an honesty of expression much used in later modern architecture.

The Gamble House provided an opportunity for a fully integrated design encompassing landscape, fixed and free-standing furniture, rugs, colored glass, light fixtures, and even electrical switches.

ROBIE HOUSE

THE ROBIE HOUSE (1908–10) in South Woodlawn, Chicago, Illinois, draws its influence from the flat plains of the American Midwest and epitomizes the domestic style of Frank Lloyd Wright's Prairie House period. These houses are spatially innovative but reassuringly solid, and were well suited to the conservative propriety of Wright's newly affluent suburban clients. The buildings have a strong axiality and openness, with the hearth forming the central feature and pivotal point to the plan. Robie House is raised above the ground on a substantial plinth; the massing emphasizes the horizontal, using the architectural order of plinth, low elevation, and deeply overhanging eaves. Wright embraced technology: connective heating, electric lighting, and rudimentary air-conditioning were adapted to service the domestic interior. While many of the Arts and Crafts architects had rejected the machine, Wright experimented with its potential for precision by incorporating highly finished surfaces, enriched by colored glass and polished timbers.

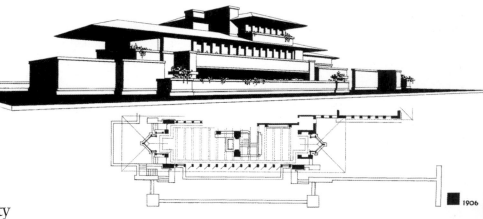

Plan

The principal spaces of the house are essentially open. Areas for different functions are defined by latticed screens and the central, controlling, position of the hearth and stairs. This fluid relationship, incorporating a subtle distinction within a sequence of spaces, is the most dynamic element of Wright's work, contributing to modern architecture's preoccupation with space and volume.

SPECIFICATION

- **Location**   Chicago, Illinois
- **Date**   1908–10
- **Architect**   Frank Lloyd Wright
- **Building structure**   Steel-frame and brick
- **Building type**   House

WINDOW BAY
The prow-like form of the window bay has a proudly nautical feel. Wright's style was likened to that of steamships, a dynamic image of the Machine Age that Wright was happy to adopt.

PLANTING BOXES
The planting boxes are discreetly fitted with irrigation sprinklers operated from a central valve – a typical example of Wright's integration of modern technology.

CANTILEVERED ROOF
The cantilever of the entrance porch is supported by steel beams, providing a distinctive silhouette. The reassuring image of the sheltering roof is used for dramatic effect in this reinterpretation of vernacular form.

ROMAN BRICKS
The slender profile of elongated, or "Roman," bricks was originally accentuated by raked mortar courses, which set back the mortar from the face of the brick, creating a shadow line that reinforced the horizontality of the massing.

Open Planning
The fireplace divides the living areas of the elevated first floor, and the screen walls provide privacy. The furniture and fittings were specifically designed for the house, and the electrical fittings and heating system are integrated into the fabric of the house.

Covered Porch
The covered porch mediates between the building's interior and exterior, extending the living space of the house. The building is elevated above street level and partially screened; this arrangement provides privacy for the occupants and allows a subtle extension of the external spaces adjacent to the house.

FRANK LLOYD WRIGHT

Frank Lloyd Wright (1867–1959) was inspired by a love of nature and the landscape of the Midwest. He began a prolific career with a style that infused vernacular architecture with new technology. Driven by a utopian spirit, Wright continually reinvented his style in domestic, commercial, and civic buildings. His astounding variety of work profoundly influenced the course of 20th-century architecture.

CHIMNEY
The chimney provides an anchoring feature central to the plan and massing of the house.

BEDROOMS
The bedrooms are tucked under the low-pitched roof, utilizing the roof space and providing a suite of private rooms that are more informal than those on lower floors.

RAISED FIRST FLOOR
The main living spaces are arranged on a raised first floor. The veranda and low walls form a series of tiered screens that provide both privacy and an open aspect from the house.

DECORATION
The colored glass and leaded lights provide a richness of detail and restrained ornamentation, which Wright considered an integral and "constituent" part of the architecture.

BRICK PIERS
The structural arrangement of load-bearing brick piers allows the walls to be inset with opening doors. Light and air permeate the interiors, extending the living space on to porches with views of the garden.

STONE VASES
Stone vases placed on the screen walls define the outer edge of the house under the projecting eaves. They emphasize the horizontality of the massing and hold the corners.

CASTLE DROGO

CASTLE DROGO (1910–30) emerges dramatically, like a medieval castle in abstracted, monumental form, from a granite outcrop 200 feet (61 meters) above the River Teign in Devon, England. Designed by Sir Edwin Lutyens, it derives much of its authenticity and boldness of composition from revisions made to the original design, which greatly reduced its scale. The omission of additional wings and a central court, which would have balanced the composition of the southern elevation, encourages the illusion of an authentic feudal castle, modified by rebuilding and organically rooted in its site. Lutyens's adherence to tradition in the use of vernacular materials and his willingness to reinterpret traditional forms define a middle ground in contrast to the radical departures of early-20th-century modern architecture. The skillful management of plan and three-dimensional form reconciles a formal grandeur with the intimate spaces of domestic architecture.

Lutyens had the form of the building partially erected as a timber and canvas mock-up, in order to gauge its completed impact and position on the site. As the original budget of about £60,000 began to escalate, the client requested a curtailment of the scale of the project, requiring continual revisions. The final building constitutes one-third of the full proposal.

Bathroom
The skylighted bathroom of the third-floor master bedroom has a Classical simplicity and introduces domestic comforts into an imposing building. The domestic apartments have an intimacy quite apart from the grandeur of the principal reception rooms.

ANGULAR DETAILING
The mass of the 4-foot- (1.2-meter-) thick granite walls is emphasized by angular detailing and the deep recession of the window openings.

SPECIFICATION

- **Location** — Devon, England
- **Date** — 1910–30
- **Architect** — Sir Edwin Lutyens
- **Building structure** — Granite and timber
- **Building type** — Castle

MULLIONED WINDOWS
The stone-mullioned windows recall the bays of Elizabethan fortified houses. They carefully order the composition of the façade and command impressive views over the dramatic landscape.

SLOPING WALLS
The upper sections of the walls are inclined, stepping back in tiered courses, giving a distinctive sculptural definition to the bat-eared towers and parapet detailing. This vernacular device, utilized for its sculptural effect, is typical of Lutyens's personalization of vernacular forms.

East Elevation

Castle Drogo is prominently positioned on the edge of a steep escarpment and forms a dramatic intermediary between land and sky. The client had sought a medieval Romanticism, which Lutyens was able to interpret in rugged detail and sculptural form.

GRANITE WALLS
Rising from the steep escarpment, the granite walls merge the form of the building with the rocky outcrop, culminating in the distinct sharpness of detailing at the skyline.

THIRD FLOOR
The private apartments, guest rooms, and nursery are located on the third floor.

CONSTRUCTION
After the first year of construction, every stone was laid by just two men. These two masons worked under the direction of a master mason in the authentic tradition of medieval construction.

Stepped Levels

Movement through the house is carefully managed between the stepped levels. The stone-vaulted corridors and staircases provide a varied sequence of circulation spaces that gracefully connect principal areas of the house.

NORTH WING
The splayed north wing follows the contour of the site and houses the bedrooms and lower-ground-floor kitchens.

SIR EDWIN LUTYENS

Sir Edwin Landseer Lutyens (1869–1944) developed a highly personal style in the many commissions for private houses designed in the manner of the English Arts and Crafts Movement. Later commissions for civic works, including the Viceroy's House (1912–31) in New Delhi and the Cenotaph (1919) in London, adopted a Neoclassical style suited to the grand plan. Lutyens's work is memorable for its skillful manipulation of the plan, affinity for the site, and versatile architectural vocabulary.

DINING ROOM
The dining room and service wing are on the ground floor, tucked into the slope of the hillside.

STEPPED SECTION
The house is situated on the edge of a steep slope and has a stepped section, with the main entrance and principal rooms on the upper-ground-floor, accessible from the court of the entrance elevation.

SCHRÖDER HOUSE

THE SCHRÖDER HOUSE (1923–24) in Utrecht was designed by Gerrit Rietveld and his client, Truus Schröder-Schrader. As with the Villa Savoye (see p. 84) and the Farnsworth House (see p. 90), it provides, within its modest scale (a two-story, end-of-terrace house), a succinct essay on some of the defining principles of early modern architecture. Rietveld was a member of De Stijl (The Style), a group of Dutch artists whose ideas about the link between art and life were influential in post-World War I Europe. Its members sought a new mode of expression in geometric forms. This house is a volumetric composition of sliding and overlapping planes slotted into the coordinates of a three-dimensional grid, thus extending the possibilities explored in painter Piet Mondrian's (1872–1944) abstract use of space and color. For De Stijl, it was part of a revolutionary package of ideas; for modern architecture, it pointed to the use of architectural elements to delineate, rather than enclose, space. The design challenges the conventional arrangement of static rooms and formal façades, allowing an overlap of functions and a fluid sequence of spaces relevant to the needs of a contemporary house and work space.

Setting
The house forms the end of an existing terrace in a complete contradiction of its contextual setting. The assertive and revolutionary tone of De Stijl sought to confront rather than defer to established conventions.

DE STIJL

The De Stijl group, formed in Holland in 1917 around the publications of the theorist and architect Theo van Doesburg, sought to liberate art through abstraction and purity of form and color, as exemplified in the work of its leading painter, Piet Mondrian. Their ideas developed through a period of continual experimentation, making an important contribution to the debate of the Modern Movement and eventually becoming absorbed into the teaching of the German Bauhaus. Unlike later Cubist-inspired architecture, De Stijl architecture found few occasions for realization, and the group's ideas are more frequently represented in painting, typography, and furniture design.

THREE-DIMENSIONAL GRID
The notion of infinite three-dimensional space is represented in the planes, edges, and vertices of the rectilinear forms, composed in primary colors, gray, black, and white.

The house is consistent in every detail – furniture, handrails, even light fixtures – making it a completely autonomous work of art, consistent with the ambitions of De Stijl.

The Red–Blue Chair
Rietveld's Red–Blue Chair (1918) is a clear statement of the principles of spatial abstraction. The overlapping frame, representing a continuous, three-dimensional grid, supports the hovering planes of the seat and back.

PLANAR GEOMETRY
The assembling of perpendicular planes to define the form and delineate spaces deconstructs the conventional cubic volumes of architectural form. The composition gives an impression of the weightless suspension of abstract elements.

PORCH SEAT
The porch seat forms an integral part of the architectural composition, as do all elements of the fixed and freestanding furniture.

GERRIT RIETVELD

After apprenticeship to his father as a furniture designer, Gerrit Rietveld (1888–1964) opened his own cabinet-making business in 1911. Rietveld studied architecture and was introduced to Theo van Doesburg and the ideas of the De Stijl group. He collaborated with Truus Schröder-Schrader on a limited number of projects that brought the spatial and abstract concerns of De Stijl to the utilities of domestic living. Although few architectural projects of De Stijl survive, Rietveld's furniture epitomizes the experimental nature of the Dutch school, which exerted a considerable influence on 20th-century art and design.

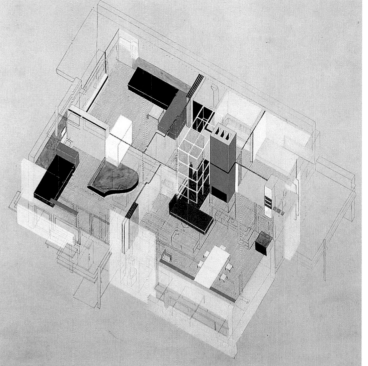

Isometric Projection

The sculptural arrangement is continued throughout the interior. The principal areas for working, relaxing, and sleeping are on the second floor, in an ambiguous and flexible series of spaces temporarily defined by movable partitions. Officially designated an attic, the second floor was not subject to the same statutory building regulations as the first floor.

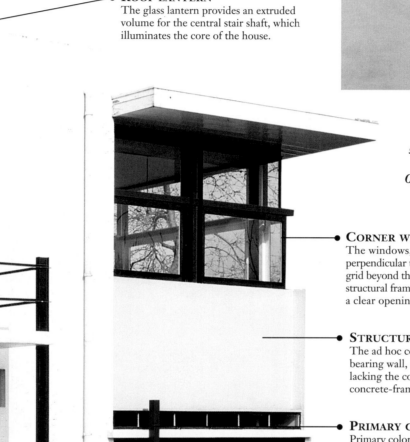

ROOF LANTERN
The glass lantern provides an extruded volume for the central stair shaft, which illuminates the core of the house.

CORNER WINDOW
The windows, when open, are held at an angle perpendicular to that of the frame, expanding the geometric grid beyond the building envelope. The window, with the structural frame set back from the corner, pivots to reveal a clear opening at the defining edge of the building.

STRUCTURAL FRAME
The ad hoc combination of structural systems, load-bearing wall, and steel frame is used for visual effect, lacking the constructional clarity of Le Corbusier's concrete-framed Dom-ino house (see p. 84).

PRIMARY COLORS
Primary colors are used to distinguish isolated elements of the frame, highlighting them as coordinates in an expanding spatial grid. The house has an abstract sculptural composition, destroying the conventions of a rectilinear box.

OVERLAPPING PLANES
Walls meet in a series of overlapping planes, expressing the composition of separate forms.

FIRST FLOOR
More conventional in arrangement than that of the second floor, the plan of the first floor was determined by the need to conform to statutory building codes and accommodates a study, the kitchen, and two bedrooms.

BALCONY SUPPORT
The steel joist provides necessary support for the concrete slab of the balcony, but is also an integral part of the sculptural composition, extending the frame of the building beyond the external walls.

SPECIFICATION

- *Location*   Utrecht, Holland
- *Date*   1923–24
- *Architects*   Gerrit Rietveld, Truus Schröder-Schrader
- *Building structure*   Steel-frame, load-bearing brick, and concrete
- *Building type*   House

VILLA SAVOYE

BY 1928, LE CORBUSIER'S PUBLICATIONS and early commissions for villas and apartments had found favor among the French bourgeoisie, putting him at the center of the avant-garde. His ideas for multistory housing, civic buildings, and urban planning were developing into a radical manifesto, consolidating his influence and shaping the course of modern architecture in the years following World War II. However, it was in the early villa commissions that these ideas were to find expression, in the novel forms and industrial materials that became associated with the Modern Movement. The Villa Savoye (1928–31) in Poissy, France, was commissioned as a weekend country house. Unlike earlier villa commissions, the unrestricted site gave Le Corbusier an opportunity to indulge his preference for the square plan as a pure and natural form. The building expresses his ambition to redefine habitable space, emphasizing volume and natural light. It concluded a period of Purist experimentation, with later projects maturing into the complex sculptural style seen at Ronchamp.

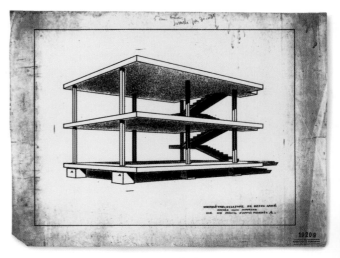

Dom-ino Skeleton
Le Corbusier recognized the architectural possibilities created by the simple skeletal form of framed structures. Concrete-slab floors, separated by columns inset from the walls, allowed the plan to develop freely within the structural grid. The walls (solid, glazed, or open) become nonstructural, used purely as an envelope to express the Purist form. The Dom-ino system (1914–15) facilitated Le Corbusier's Five Points for a New Architecture *(1926): a free plan; pilotis; a free facade; ribbon windows; and a roof garden.*

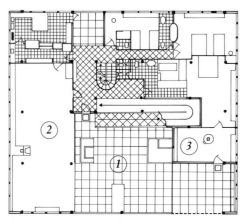

Second-floor Plan
The second-floor terrace (1) is enclosed by the screen wall, glimpsed from the exterior through the ribbon windows continued through the façade. Treated as an outside room, and a clear extension of the living area, the terrace connects to the main living room (2) by sliding glass doors. The bedroom (3) also opens onto the terrace, allowing movement between spaces that overlap in use and definition.

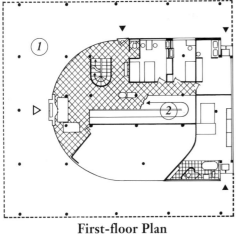

First-floor Plan
The U-shaped first-floor plan of the reception and service areas was designed to accommodate the turning circle (1) of a car delivering occupants to the door and to continue this flow of movement to the internal ramp (2), which sweeps up through the principal public spaces, terminating at the rooftop sun terrace.

CURVILINEAR FORMS
The curvilinear forms of the roof garden resemble the geometry of Cubist painting and sculpture. The funnel-like forms also evoke the nautical imagery of ocean liners.

PILOTI
Piloti are slender columns forming the structural frame, which elevates the main living area (*piano nobile*) above the ground.

Le Corbusier celebrated the 20th century and the objects of an industrialized society – the steamship, airplane, and car – comparing their engineers to the greatest Classical architects.

PIANO NOBILE
Le Corbusier adopted the *piano nobile* from the palazzos of the Italian Renaissance. The main living area is raised above the ground level and provides views from terraces and balconies.

LE CORBUSIER

Le Corbusier (1887–1966) dominated and encompassed the goals of the Modern Movement. The functional requirements of modern society led him famously to offer the analogy of the house as "a machine for living." He aimed to realign construction and design to progressive industrial methods, combining the planar, abstract geometry of Cubist theory with simple and unadorned forms of rendered concrete and plate glass. Later he pursued sculptural form and poetic simplicity. His buildings demonstrate the potential of simple and radical architecture.

NOTRE-DAME-DU-HAUT

The pilgrimage chapel at Notre-Dame-du-Haut, Ronchamp (1950–54), in the Vosges mountains in France, illustrates the maturity of Le Corbusier's late work – distanced by World War II from Purism and the machine aesthetic. The hull-like form of the concrete-shell roof is supported in a frame of reinforced concrete, concealed within the curved and tapering walls. The eastern wall, pierced by deeply set, colored windows, projects to the edge of the roof canopy in a sheltering curve, which protects the altar and pulpit used in the alfresco celebration of Mass. This sculptural device turns the building inside out, providing a nave of grass and a backdrop of distant views.

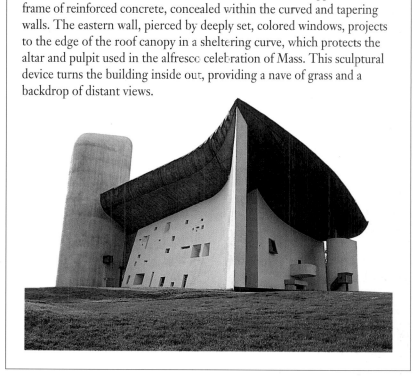

ROOF GARDEN
The flat roof emphasizes the planar, Cubist geometry, allowing the roof to become a garden and sun terrace.

WHITE EXTERIOR
The white "ocean-liner" exterior contrasts with the interior spaces, often composed in planes of solid color.

SPECIFICATION

- **Location** — Poissy, France
- **Date** — 1928–31
- **Architect** — Le Corbusier
- **Building structure** — Concrete-frame
- **Building type** — Villa
- **Construction time** — 3 years

RIBBON WINDOW
Unrestricted by conventional load-bearing walls, the window continues along the length of the façade, even turning the corner, allowing a framed view of the horizon and giving a strong horizontal emphasis to the building.

Methods of industrial production and standardized components were considered desirable by Le Corbusier. However, machine finishes were often achieved through intensive labor skills. In this respect, architectural construction was, for example, far behind the industrial methods common in the auto industry.

FREE FACADE
The set-back of the perimeter columns from the edge of the wall allows the main, framed structure to be internal. The perimeter wall acts as a *curtain* that can be drawn taut to express the geometry of the cube, or opened, to maximize natural light.

"Architecture is the masterly, correct, and magnificent play of masses brought together in light"
LE CORBUSIER

COMPOSITION
The building, when viewed from the edge of the site, is seen as free-standing and carefully composed, rather like a Palladian villa, such as the Villa Rotonda (see p. 48).

EMPIRE STATE BUILDING

THE EMPIRE STATE BUILDING (1929–31) was designed by R. H. Shreve, T. Lamb, and A. L. Harmon and is an example of the skyscrapers of the glittering interwar years, before the sobriety of Depression-era New Deal America. At 1,250 feet (381 meters) and 102 stories, it succeeded to the title of the world's tallest building in 1931, a title previously held by the nearby Chrysler Building, which is 1,046 feet (319 meters) tall. The rapid growth of midtown New York, supported by a large commuting workforce, had increased the density of city development, raising the value of city plots. Developments in lighting, heating, plumbing, ventilation, mechanical excavation, foundation design, and fireproofing responded to the demand for increased building height. Clients were greatly attracted to this conspicuous form of construction and competed for prominence in the city skyline. The public was captivated by the excitement of the Jazz Age and the ever increasing confection of architectural style. Completed during the worst years of the Great Depression, the building remained empty for many years.

Construction
Using new technology and site-management techniques, the building was driven up at a rate of four and a half stories a week by 3,500 site workers. The construction took 410 days from groundbreak to handover, at one point achieving over 14 stories in 10 days.

Steel-framed Construction
By the end of the 19th century, engineers were familiar with steel-framed construction for engineering and industrial structures, such as bridges and railroad stations. The early 20th century saw the exploitation of this construction method for multistory buildings.

MAST TOWER
The top 30 stories are lit with a changing sequence of colored lights, marking national holidays and major events. Three thousand visitors a day flocked to the observation deck in the initial years of underoccupation, generating a yearly income of $1 million, an important revenue following the stock market crash of 1929.

LANDING STAGE
The 16-story steel mast tower houses the observation deck and was designed as a mooring mast for blimps. It was used only twice as a "dock," but the progressive image of the skyscraper as a lighthouse reached by blimp offered a futuristic image of modernity.

STRUCTURE
The 350,000-ton (365,000-tonne) building uses 10 million bricks on a 59,000-ton (60,000-tonne) riveted steel structure. The Empire State remained the world's tallest building until 1973, when it was superseded by the World Trade Center.

ELEVATORS
Technical developments in the speed and increased travel distance of the passenger elevator enabled practical occupation of multistory buildings. The building has a total of 62 elevators, arranged in core clusters.

SPECIFICATION

•Location	New York, New York
•Date	1929–31
•Architects	R. H. Shreve, T. Lamb, A. L. Harmon
•Height	1,250 ft (381 m)
•Stories	102
•Building structure	Steel-frame
•Building type	Offices
•Construction time	58 weeks

Zoning Laws
The New York Zoning Ordinance Laws of 1916 sought to regulate city development. Buildings were subject to rules that, by mandating increasingly deeper setbacks as a building rose higher above the street, allowed more light to reach the ground level and afforded better lighting to the ascending floors. Hugh Ferris's drawing (1929) illustrates the maximum permitted volume conforming to the codes.

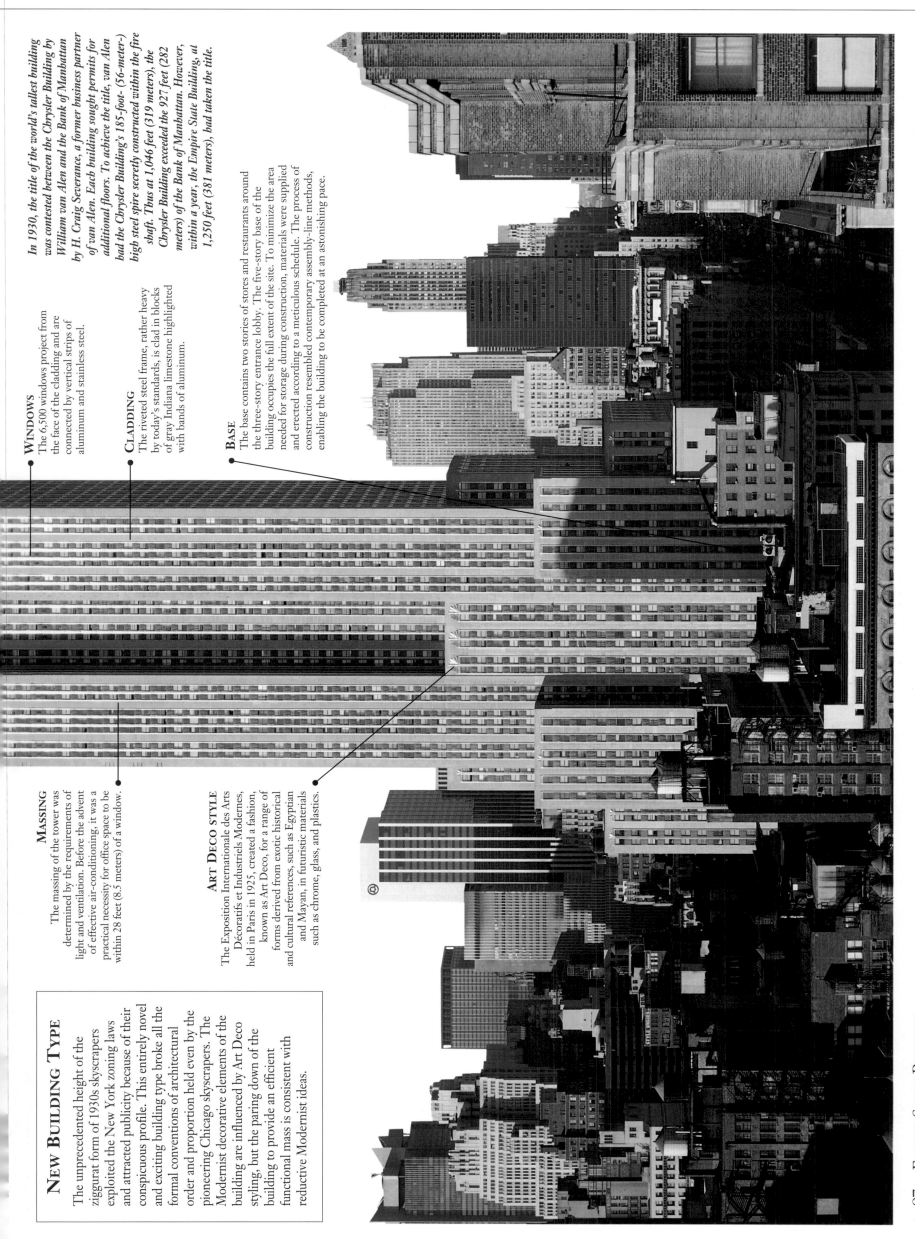

New Building Type

The unprecedented height of the ziggurat-form of 1930s skyscrapers exploited the New York zoning laws and attracted publicity because of their conspicuous profile. This entirely novel and exciting building type broke all the formal conventions of architectural order and proportion held even by the pioneering Chicago skyscrapers. The Modernist decorative elements of the building are influenced by Art Deco styling, but the paring down of the building to provide an efficient functional mass is consistent with reductive Modernist ideas.

MASSING
The massing of the tower was determined by the requirements of light and ventilation. Before the advent of effective air-conditioning, it was a practical necessity for office space to be within 28 feet (8.5 meters) of a window.

ART DECO STYLE
The Exposition Internationale des Arts Décoratifs et Industriels Modernes, held in Paris in 1925, created a fashion, known as Art Deco, for a range of forms derived from exotic historical and cultural references, such as Egyptian and Mayan, in futuristic materials such as chrome, glass, and plastics.

WINDOWS
The 6,500 windows project from the face of the cladding and are connected by vertical strips of aluminum and stainless steel.

CLADDING
The riveted steel frame, rather heavy by today's standards, is clad in blocks of gray Indiana limestone highlighted with bands of aluminum.

BASE
The base contains two stories of stores and restaurants around the three-story entrance lobby. The five-story base of the building occupies the full extent of the site. To minimize the area needed for storage during construction, materials were supplied and erected according to a meticulous schedule. The process of construction resembled contemporary assembly-line methods, enabling the building to be completed at an astonishing pace.

In 1930, the title of the world's tallest building was contested between the Chrysler Building by William van Alen and the Bank of Manhattan by H. Craig Severance, a former business partner of van Alen. Each building sought permits for additional floors. To achieve the title, van Alen had the Chrysler Building's 185-foot- (56-meter-) high steel spire secretly constructed within the fire shaft. Thus at 1,046 feet (319 meters), the Chrysler Building exceeded the 927 feet (282 meters) of the Bank of Manhattan. However, within a year, the Empire State Building, at 1,250 feet (381 meters), had taken the title.

VILLA MAIREA

BY THE MID-1930S, the Modern Movement had begun a new phase. Early experimentation with Purist form, new materials, and machine finishes (typified by Le Corbusier's Villa Savoye [see p. 84] and the development of the International Style) had shifted toward establishing regional identities, absorbing local traditions, and responding to specific climatic and cultural preferences. The Villa Mairea (1938–41) was commissioned as a private residence. Set amid the beauty of the forest in Noormarkku, Finland, it expresses the developing maturity of the Modern Movement. Alvar Aalto brought the Modernist preoccupation with open space, natural light, and sculptural form to a contemporary use of local crafts and building skills. The house achieves a strong sense of connection with its situation and Finnish cultural traditions, blending the surviving traditions and vernacular rustication with the simple restraint of Nordic Classicism.

Garden and Pool
The L-shaped plan of the villa shelters the garden and swimming pool to the rear. The glass screens allow direct connection with the garden terrace and views of the forest. The screens and simple timber detailing illustrate Aalto's interest in Japanese architecture.

COLUMN SPANS
The column spans are varied in order to break away from the monotony of the building grid. In this respect, the building has an informal relationship with structure, unlike Le Corbusier's regulated Dom-ino plan or the disciplined grid of Mies van der Rohe.

TIMBER BOARDS
The studio wing is paneled with vertical boards. The profile of the timber slats emphasizes both the curved volume of the studio wall and the grain of the timber.

HANDRAIL
The "ship's handrail" above the balcony is a familiar Modernist motif and is detailed in both tubular steel and natural-grained timber.

ALVAR AALTO

The early designs of Alvar Aalto (1898–1976) established his reputation as one of the major exponents of early International Modernist architecture. His work expresses the Finnish traditions of simple Classicism, affinity for natural materials, and fine use of indigenous craft skills. His architectural commissions and designs for furniture and glassware consolidated his contribution as one of the most influential of 20th-century architects.

NATURAL MATERIALS
The ground-floor library is clad in teak boards, with the lower junctions near the ground paneled in granite. Each has a richly toned self-color, adding to the collage of materials on the façade.

PLANTING
The brackets set between the stone panels support wires for awnings and a plant-watering conduit. Climbing plants are encouraged as further textural materials in areas of the façade.

Covered Terrace

A paved terrace, covered by a timber canopy with a turf roof, leads from the main house to the detached sauna. The rustic materials, such as the woven door and wicker binding, create a naturalized, softened edge with the landscape.

The Fireplace

The hearth provides a simple focus to many of the rooms. The dining-room fireplace, contrasting the exposed brick with white plaster, terminates a view through the open plan of the living areas from the entrance porch. The fireplace chimney is shared by an outside fireplace on the covered terrace, which backs onto the dining room.

STRUCTURE

The upper bedrooms are supported on a system of columns and load-bearing walls. The columns vary in material and position, and are chosen with regard to the room size, rather than being determined by the regular intervals of the constructional frame.

BAY WINDOWS

With their triangular plan, the bay windows provide striking views directed towards the landscaped forest approach. The building is adjusted to the site, giving prominence to views out to the grounds.

TEXTURAL FINISH

The bedroom and studio wings have a white, volumetric form familiar to Modern Movement buildings, but here the smooth white render of modern Cubist architecture is complemented by areas of lime-washed brick, having a textural and rusticated surface.

"Nature, not the machine, is the most important model for architecture"
ALVAR AALTO

Handcrafted wood, ceramics, and glass contribute to the characteristic richness and simplicity of Scandinavian design. The skills needed in these crafts, maintained in unbroken tradition, had survived the process of industrialization, becoming absorbed into the rustic tendencies of late Modernism.

ENTRANCE PORCH

The entrance porch has a free-form timber canopy supported by eccentrically placed columns and a timber screen – in reference to the prevailing image of the sheltering forest.

SPECIFICATION

•*Location*	Noormarkku, Finland
•*Date*	1938–41
•*Architect*	Alvar Aalto
•*Building structure*	Reinforced concrete, brick, stone, timber, and steel
•*Storeys*	2
•*Building type*	Villa

FARNSWORTH HOUSE

IN CONTRAST TO THE LATER sculptural and rusticated tendencies of Modernist architecture exemplified by Le Corbusier (see p. 84) and Alvar Aalto (see p. 88), Ludwig Mies van der Rohe was to pursue a disciplined course of Modernism, exploring the minimalist possibilities of the structural-steel frame and the transparency of the glass box – an image summarized by his phrase "less is more." Mies van der Rohe set the trend for the corporate architecture of the high-rise office building, but few exponents achieve the almost abstract beauty of his late work, which combines a rigorous organizing structure with a fastidious attention to proportion and constructional detail. The Farnsworth House (1945–51), standing on the north bank of the Fox River, 60 miles (96.5 kilometers) from Chicago, Illinois, provides a sophisticated and ascetic place of retreat from urban life, as had Villa Rotonda (see p. 48) four centuries earlier. Like the Villa Rotonda, it shows its lineage from Classical Greek temples, but achieved here in a thoroughly mid-20th-century idiom. The pristine white frame, set amid the "Arcadian landscape," is a definitive expression of cool Modernism and Classical simplicity.

SPECIFICATION

- **Location**   Chicago, Illinois
- **Date**   1945–51
- **Architect**   Ludwig Mies van der Rohe
- **Building structure**   Welded steel-frame
- **Building type**   House

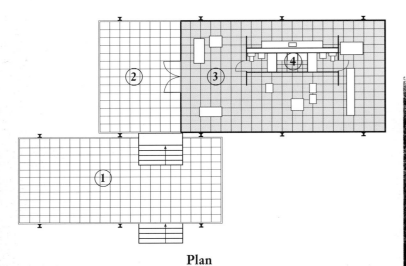

Plan
The plan allows the maximum transparency and views to the landscape. There are three connected areas: an open, raised deck (1); a covered porch (2); and a glass enclosure (3). The service core (4) contains two bathrooms, the kitchen, a fireplace, and a storage unit. The concentration of storage and services in the central core frees the exterior from the interference of pipes and wires, maintaining its simplicity of form.

PRISTINE FRAME
The zinc-coated steel frame is covered with white enamel paint, polished to a high finish. It thus hides any marks of fabrication.

ELEVATED STEEL FRAME
The exposed steel frame elevates the floor 4 feet (1.2 meters) above the ground, visually detaching the building from the landscape.

Interior
The bathroom and storage core is concealed behind an arrangement of non-load-bearing partitions, allowing the occupant to presume a life of monastic simplicity. The partitions provide a flexible interior, subtly distinguishing between areas loosely designated for living, sleeping, and eating.

MARBLE SLABS
The marble slabs have a concealed drainage detail, enabling them to be laid completely flat and thus maintaining the precision and alignment of the horizontal plane.

The house was commissioned by Edith Farnsworth as a weekend retreat. Despite proclaiming dissatisfaction with the finished result, she continued to occupy the house for 17 years.

LUDWIG MIES VAN DER ROHE

Mies van der Rohe (1886–1969) achieved prominence with his crystalline skyscraper designs in 1919. The Barcelona Pavilion (1928–29) and the Seagram Building (1954–58), New York, exemplify the cool Modernism of the single-story pavilion and the high-rise office building, exerting a lasting influence on the Modern Movement.

CONCEALED FIXTURES
The steel frame is welded to a high degree of accuracy and workmanship. The welds are meticulously ground off and all other fixtures fastidiously concealed.

Minimalism
The understated elegance of the frame and glazing is achieved through careful attention to detail. To maintain this elemental simplicity, all the services, drainage, and fixtures must be carefully coordinated and controlled. Mies van der Rohe's extremely reductive style helped create the architectural genre known as Minimalism.

PLATE-GLASS WINDOWS
The full-length plate glass of the windows is set between the structural-steel frame and secured by a minimal steel glazing bead. Cross-ventilation is provided by the doors and one opening window.

TRANSPARENCY
The addition of silk curtains to screen and shade the interior, following the building of a road and a river crossing that overlook the house, has resulted in the loss of the transparency of the glass box.

STAIR TREADS
The travertine marble that is used for the floor deck is also used for the stair treads, which are similarly detailed as hovering horizontal planes.

SYDNEY OPERA HOUSE

THE OPERA HOUSE ON THE PROMINENT waterfront site of Sydney Harbor has become one of modern architecture's most popular icons. The competition-winning design of 1957, by Jørn Utzon, was awarded on the strength of the conceptual ideas he submitted in outline sketch proposals. The building employs three important elements: a hovering roof structure facilitating public functions; a podium housing the support facilities; and a terraced concourse incorporating the processional routes that link the spaces designed for social gathering. The sail-like, floating roof shells, which rise from the massive, tiered podium, seem to emerge dramatically from the water and are reminiscent of the waterside Gothic churches of Utzon's native Denmark and the yachts in full sail that fill Sydney Harbor. Indeed, it is the latter image that succeeds in the executed design – which ultimately overwhelmed the technical problems experienced in matching form to function. Changes to the design and protracted delays led to Utzon's resignation. The building was completed – at ten times the original budget – by the team of Hall, Littlemore, and Todd in 1973.

Aerial View
Sydney Opera House stands on the headland of Bennelong Point in Sydney Harbor. The three main clusters of interlocking concrete shells, with an inclined central axis converging toward the landward approach, accommodate two main halls (one for opera and one for concert performances), a movie house (originally a theater), and a restaurant.

SPECIFICATION

- **Location**   Sydney, Australia
- **Date**   1959–73
- **Architect**   Jørn Utzon
- **Building structure**   Reinforced concrete vaults with concrete shell covering
- **Building type**   Concert hall
- **Constuction time**   14 years

GLAZING
The open ends of the shells are enclosed within suspended glass panels.

INTERLOCKING SHELLS
The interlocking shell clusters are generated from segments of a single sphere, providing a common curvature and helping to simplify the complex resolution of joints and cladding components.

SHELLS
The shells are formed from a combination of prefabricated and cast-*in-situ* concrete. The precast-concrete ribs are glued together in sections, radiating from the central concrete pedestals. The Y-sectioned ribs are laterally strung together with prestressed-steel tie rods and supported at the outward ends by concrete edge beams.

PROCESSIONAL ROUTE
The podium has three tiers, providing a processional route up wide flights of steps toward the entrances to the auditoriums, which are approached from the main public concourse.

SHELL SEGMENTS
The shell segments, up to 197 feet (60 meters) high, are made from ribbed and radiating concrete beams with a 2-inch- (5-centimeter-) thick shell wall.

Because scenery is raised from beneath the main stage, the conventional bulk of traditional opera houses, which have large fly towers for scenery changes, is avoided.

Acoustic Environment

The form of the shell structure posed a number of problems for the functional requirements of the concert hall. Plywood panels line the interior, modifying the acoustic environment. Plexiglas panels, seen from above the stage, can be lowered to provide reflective surfaces for sound projection.

Speaking about the notion of Additive Architecture (see box), Utzon cited Alvar Aalto's example of cherry blossoms: "each blossom [is] different from its neighbor according to its special position on the branch, but all the blossoms [are] composed of the same elements. ... [This is] the foundation of many of my projects."

Jørn Utzon

Jørn Utzon (b. 1918) was born in Copenhagen, Denmark. He worked for two influential modern Scandinavian architects: Gunar Asplund (1885–1940) and Alvar Aalto (see p. 88). Utzon's designs are characterized by clear and conceptual statements that generate simple solutions – often from a "family of related objects." This concept became known as *Additive Architecture*.

Concert hall

The main concert hall is enclosed within the highest shell section. Originally, the proposal called for a dual-purpose hall that could accommodate both orchestral and operatic performances. The concert hall has 2,900 seats.

Opera theater

Problems arising from conflicting acoustic and programmatic requirements led to the provision of a separate opera theater. This theater has 1,547 seats.

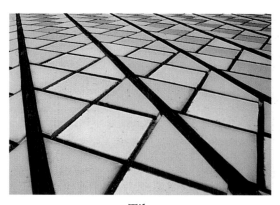

Tiles

The precast-concrete rib vaults are clad in a combination of over one million glazed and matte ceramic tiles. The tiles accentuate the radial pattern of the building and glisten in the light like fish scales.

Utzon uses the device of served and servant spaces (characteristic of late modern architecture) in the design of the building. Servant areas within the podium, such as kitchens and offices, provide functions that sustain the activities within the prominent served areas of the building, such as the walkways, auditoriums, and foyers.

Podium

The concrete-framed podium contains all the support facilities, with the main public spaces placed above ground, allowing uninterrupted views across the harbor.

Cladding

The podium is clad in granite panels, emphasizing its mass and providing a visually supportive base for the soaring, lightweight roof shells, which are clad in white ceramic tiles.

The functional requirement of accommodating the shell structure to the form of the interior posed many design problems and required subsequent revisions of the seating capacity.

TOKYO OLYMPIC STADIUM

IN THE SIMPLE, FORMAL, and spiritually resonant qualities of traditional Japanese design, the early-20th-century Modernists were able to recognize a prototype for the language of modern architecture. These intrinsic qualities form part of a national cultural heritage, which Japan continues to exert with influence on contemporary architecture. Designed by Kenzo Tange for the swimming and basketball events of the 1964 Tokyo Olympic Games, the Tokyo Olympic Stadium (1961–64) is a skillful resolution of complex functions demonstrated with disarming simplicity and sculptural clarity. The project has three distinct elements: a large and a small stadium linked by a service building whose flat roof doubles as a walkway across the site. The dramatic form provides a seamless integration of function and structure and conveys the symbolism and eloquence of traditional Japanese architecture. It succeeds because it goes beyond the realm of mere functionalism. It offers a simple and poetic image to reinterpret the coolly rational principle of "form follows function" and epitomizes Tange's assertion that only something that is beautiful can be truly functional.

Roof Form
The oversailing canopy of the main stadium offers an unambiguous and welcoming point of arrival. The form of the roof naturally shelters and funnels spectators into the stadium without disturbing activity in the arena. The articulation of form and function is assisted by the sculptural form of the building.

SPECIFICATION

- **Location**   Tokyo, Japan
- **Date**   1961–64
- **Architect**   Kenzo Tange
- **Building structure**   Reinforced concrete, steel, and tensile structure
- **Building type**   Sports stadium

CONCRETE MAST
The concrete mast forms a cradle supporting the main roof cables. The simple detailing makes a convincing and reassuring display of the means of support of such a dramatic and delicate structure.

CONTEMPORARY EXPRESSION
The forked arms of the concrete mast allude to the crossed rafters of traditional Shinto shrines (see p. 16). Although this reference is muted and intrinsic to the structure, it sufficiently establishes its unique cultural heredity.

MAIN TENSION CABLES
The deeply embedded concrete base anchors the massive tension cables, each 13 inches (33 centimeters) in diameter. Tensile structures possess a lightness of appearance, but the forces restrained by the steel cables are immense.

ANCHOR POSTS
The powerful forces of compression and tension, confronted by the concrete and steel, are dramatically conveyed at the junction of the cable and anchor posts.

ENTRANCE CANOPY
The entrance canopy is formed by the dislocation of the elliptical plan along its central axis. The symmetry of the form effortlessly accommodates the function of the plan and has a natural balance of structure.

ROOFLINE
The gentle curve of the roofline makes an oblique reference to the line of traditional Japanese temple roofs.

KENZO TANGE

The early career of Kenzo Tange (b. 1913) established a bridge between European Modernism and Japan's newly emergent culture after World War II. Tange co-founded the influential Metabolist group, which experimented with radical and flexible solutions to increasing urban density. Tange's career as architect, teacher, and urbanist has earned him an international reputation and inspired a new wave of expressive and original Japanese architecture.

Aerial View
The main stadium is elliptical in plan and seats 15,000 spectators. It contained the swimming and diving events and could also be converted into an ice-skating rink. The smaller, circular stadium, seating 4,000 people, was originally designed for basketball, but hosts other sporting events and conference facilities. The buildings are linked by a support facility that houses locker rooms, a practice pool, a dining hall, and offices. The roof provides a pedestrian causeway across the site for visitors. The elevated walkway has maintained its popularity, to become a lively space for cultural activities and public promenading.

Suspended Roof Structure
The architecture provides a dramatic backdrop to the international Olympic event without upstaging the function of the building. The pioneering form of the suspended roof provides a lightweight, clear spanning structure. The internal volume dramatically fullfils the promise of its external form, maintaining uninterrupted sight lines and directing the spectators' attention to the central competition area.

CATENARY ROOF CABLES
The catenary roof cables (hanging freely between two points of support) are tied to the main support cable. A net, produced by the weft of transverse cables, supports the steel plates covering the roof. The shape of the cables describes a complex, but natural, three-dimensional curve to the roof form.

SKYLIGHTS
The tension in the main support cables results in an elliptical opening along the ridge. This has been used to provide a louvered skylight to admit natural light to the interior.

OUTER WALL
The concrete outer wall provides a peripheral restraint to the roof-cable net. Its sculptural curve responds to the forces in the cables. The form is seemingly lifted by the tension in the roof, achieving a taut and natural poise.

ROOF PROFILE
The undulating profile of the roof is calculated to allow uninterrupted sight lines for spectators in the stadium. The seats are arranged on raked tiers, cantilevered from the concrete piers that support the outer wall.

STONE PLINTH
The stonework of the retaining walls is reminiscent of that of the massive fortifications of Japanese feudal castles. The landscaping of the terraced levels complements the sculptural form of the stadia.

EXPOSED CONCRETE
The finished quality of exposed concrete relies on the precision of the joinery needed to produce the timber formwork, making it a particularly suitable material for the meticulous standards of Japanese construction.

THE POMPIDOU CENTER

THE POMPIDOU CENTER (1971–77) is situated in the historic heart of Paris. It has achieved notoriety both for its frank industrial aesthetic and for its role in redefining the function of a civic cultural institution. Despite design revisions enforced during its construction, on its completion in 1977, it achieved popular acclaim, receiving 6 million visitors in its first year. The international competition for its design was won by the young and radical team of Renzo Piano and Richard Rogers, despite the reservations of the architectural establishment. The building was conceived as a large, free-spanning structure, designed to achieve optimum openness and flexibility, while reconciling the requirements of safety, security, and movement for huge numbers of people. The scheme concentrates the accommodation within an underground substructure and an elevated steel-framed superstructure, freeing up the ground level and thus providing an open area for public gatherings and street entertainment. The building has gallery space, a library, a movie theater, and a design center. Power and environmental controls are distributed through vents at floor and ceiling level, creating an uninterrupted, serviced environment. Its lively piazza provides a memorable experience for its many visitors, now accustomed to its unconventional appearance and radical design.

Services
The vertical tubes carrying electricity, water, drainage, and air-handling ducts are placed on the outside of the building. Boldly exposed in coded colors, their position enables accessibility for future modification while allowing flexibility of planning for the interior.

GERBERETTES
Rocker beams, called gerberettes, provide mechanical joints to the steel frame. Gerberettes are cast by spinning molten stainless steel, which allows them to be shaped to the line of forces within the beam. The scale of the span occasioned the unprecedented size of the castings. The structure uses a number of cast connections, lending the component joints a sculptural quality.

PIN JOINTS
The use of flexible pin joints within the frame prevents the overstressing of components that occurs when small movements are locked into a rigid frame.

GLASS WALLS
External glass walls screen the unprotected steel structure from the risk of internal fires. The walls are potentially removable, as they are independent of the building's structure.

PREFABRICATION
Each frame of the bay was constructed from prefabricated components and erected in 10 days. Site connections were screwed and bolted for quick assembly, with very few welded joints.

TRUSSES
Tubular steel floor trusses provide bracing between the main framing members, spanning front to back.

TIE RODS
Diagonal tie rods cross-brace the main structural frames, which comprise 14 vertical 6-story steel frames.

BLINDS
Retractable solar blinds screen the glass façades, thus shading the gallery spaces.

MAIN FRAME
The main frame is set back from the edge of the building, minimizing its impact on the façade and allowing views to and from the building through the delicate layers of structure and building envelope.

Open space for public activity and social gatherings is provided by confining the building to a part of the site that screens traffic noise and pollution from the piazza.

CONCRETE SUBSTRUCTURE
Located beneath the piazza is underground parking space for up to 700 cars, a movie theater, as well as extensive storage space and large areas for plant equipment.

Walking City

The potential for the integration into architecture of advanced technology was explored by an influential group of British architects who formed the Archigram group in 1960. The Walking City (1964), by Ron Herron, is one of a series of theoretical projects that uses Pop Art and sci-fi imagery to challenge established notions about what buildings do, whom they serve, and how they look. The Pompidou Center embodies a number of these issues.

RENZO PIANO AND RICHARD ROGERS

Renzo Piano (*left*) (see p. 106) and Richard Rogers (b. 1933) (*right*) formed a partnership in 1970, for their competition entry for the Pompidou Center. Both men are recognized for their interests in structural and technological innovation and urban design, and hold an influential position in contemporary architecture.

Structural Capabilities

To achieve its long span, the frame exploits the structural capabilities of the steelwork. Movement in the rocker beam, or gerberette, allowed by a pin passing through the main column, puts the hollow column in compression, and the vertical steel rod, gripped at the lever's outer edge, in tension.

SPECIFICATION

- **Location** — Paris, France
- **Date** — 1971–77
- **Architects** — Renzo Piano, Richard Rogers
- **Building structure** — Steel-frame and concrete
- **Stories** — 6
- **Building type** — Cultural center

ESCALATOR

The 492-foot- (150-meter-) long escalator is suspended within a toughened glass tube, slung like a lifeboat from the main structural frame. The escalator provides one of the best free views of the Parisian skyline.

The 157-foot (48-meter) span of the frame and the scale of the components required a sophisticated system for relieving stresses in the frame, caused by temperature and settlement movements between materials expanding at different rates.

FIREPROOFING

Main structural components are protected by fireproof jackets and over-cladding panels. Water sprinkler systems, activated in the event of fire, are positioned to cool the structural connections and spray the glass screens.

FIRE ESCAPE

The eight escape stairs are contained within independent steel towers.

FLOOR BEAMS

The columns, set back 23 feet (7 meters) from the building face at 43-foot (13-meter) intervals, connect to the steel-lattice floor beams that span the depth of the building.

The glass walls were originally intended to display projected images, incorporating electronic signage to convey advertising and political messages. These were omitted, however, due to concern that they could be used for propaganda.

MAIN COLUMNS

Water-filled columns cool the building in the event of fire. Open at the top, the columns would allow the water to boil off, preventing the steel from becoming flexible and collapsing.

NEUE STAATSGALERIE

THE NEUE STAATSGALERIE (1977–84) in Stuttgart, Germany, by Sir James Stirling (with Michael Wilford) is an extension to the existing Neoclassical art museum. It was inspired by 19th-century galleries, notably the Altes Museum (see p. 64), and by the form of the buildings adjacent to the site. The competition brief required a public route through the building and a raised podium to conceal car parking. The galleries are arranged in a U-shaped block, raised on a podium, with administrative offices to the rear. The central rotunda forms a sculpture court – the focal point of the gallery spaces and the public route through the site. A separate wing houses an experimental theater. Approached by a ramp from the street, the podium provides access to the free-form lobby, dramatically lit by a curved glass wall. The building quotes freely from an eclectic architectural vocabulary of Classical and Modernist forms. Stirling's virtuosic composition and rich, spatially innovative style introduce an uncompromising contemporary design into a complex, urban setting.

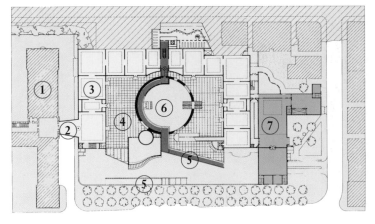

Plan

The building responds formally to the adjacent and facing buildings and to the existing galleries (1), which are connected by a bridge (2) to the gallery wings (3), forming a U-shaped plan enclosing the sculpture terrace (4). A sequence of ramps (5) brings visitors up from the street and continues a public route through the central rotunda (6) to the street at a higher level at the back of the site. A separate wing (7) houses an experimental theater.

SCULPTURE TERRACE
The public terrace flows around the free-form elements linking the separate parts of the gallery. This collage of sculptural objects is ordered against the simple backdrop of the U-shaped gallery wings.

Stirling exploits the form of the gallery to address fundamental issues of late-20th-century urban architecture – contextuality and urban space.

Blocks of Stone
The blocks of stone that appear to have tumbled from the opening in the podium wall – ventilating the parking garage – are scattered on the lawn. These stones are among the few solid blocks in the building, the façade being a thin, cladding veneer. Stirling's witty Mannerism reveals the edges of the building to expose its construction.

ARCHED WINDOWS
The Romanesque arched windows and Egyptian cornices are examples of the many motifs borrowed from a diverse architectural vocabulary.

The controversial competition proposal was criticized as monumental and overbearing, with uncomfortable associations with fascist Neoclassical architecture. Yet the completed building, though monumental and ironic, is moderated by a skillful – and playful – handling of form and detail.

Central Courtyard

Viewed from the public route, the central courtyard of the Staatsgalerie provides an active focus for the gallery spaces. The cylindrical form recalls the domed central space of Classical and Renaissance buildings. Although the building was famously criticized as "virtuosity around a void," the rotunda is a memorable and identifiable civic space. The popularity of the scheme owes much to its architectural image of being both monumental and democratic, retaining a sense of humor that is more readily Mannerist than dogmatically Modernist or, indeed, Postmodern.

SIR JAMES STIRLING

The architecture of Sir James Stirling (1926–92) demonstrates his enthusiasm for structure and technology. His eclectic range of influences are drawn from Modernist and Renaissance sources with great virtuosity and invention. Early buildings, such as Leicester University Engineering Building (1959–63), in partnership with James Gowan (b. 1923), established his reputation. Other buildings include the Cambridge University History Building (1964–67). Michael Wilford became a partner in 1971 and has continued the practice.

HANDRAILS

The brightly colored tubular-steel handrails are whimsically oversized to emphasize the circulation routes of the ramp. Other elements, such as ventilation grilles and entrance canopies, are similarly scaled-up for visual emphasis.

AEDICULA

The steel and glass canopy (aedicula) marks the central line of the building as viewed from the street. However, unlike in a conventional Classical plan, visitors are diverted from what appears to be a centrally placed entrance toward the ramped approach to the second-floor podium and entrance foyer.

The design acknowledges the form of the adjacent buildings (its context) and the precedent of the art gallery, such as Karl Friedrich Schinkel's Altes Museum (see p. 64), as a 19th-century building type.

SPECIFICATION

•*Location*	Stuttgart, Germany
•*Date*	1977–84
•*Architect*	Sir James Stirling
•*Building structure*	Masonry, steel, and reinforced concrete
•*Stories*	2
•*Building type*	Art gallery

"In addition to the representational and abstract, this large complex, I hope, supports the monumental and informal; also the traditional and hi-tech"
SIR JAMES STIRLING

ENTRANCE LOBBY

The curved entrance lobby resembles, in plan, the piano-shaped curves of many of Le Corbusier's Modernist buildings. The foyer provides an informal place of assembly for visitors, directing them toward the peripheral circulation routes of the gallery wings.

PODIUM

The podium, which conceals the ground-floor parking area, elevates the public space above the noise and pollution of the busy main road.

HONG KONG AND SHANGHAI BANK

CONSTRUCTED IN FOUR YEARS ON A RESTRICTED SITE, in scale and complexity, this building represents a remarkable technological achievement. Commissioned at a time of political uncertainty, the building is a symbol of confidence in Hong Kong's future as an international center of financial trading. Foster Associates' initial scheme was based on the concept of "phased regeneration." This would allow flexibility for the construction phases, keeping the existing bank building on the site in use until the final phase. The new building, towering over the existing bank, was to be constructed in vertical slices. This concept gave rise to the building's characteristic and identifiable superstructure. The vertical mast towers, which support the floors in tiers of office space, are suspended from the large horizontal trusses. Though the idea of phased regeneration was later abandoned in order to utilize the basement levels within the scheme, the positioning of the structural frame at either end of the floor plan allows uninterrupted, flexible planning of the office space. This flexibility is a consistent design philosophy that is used to anticipate future adaptations within the controlling organization of the building's structure.

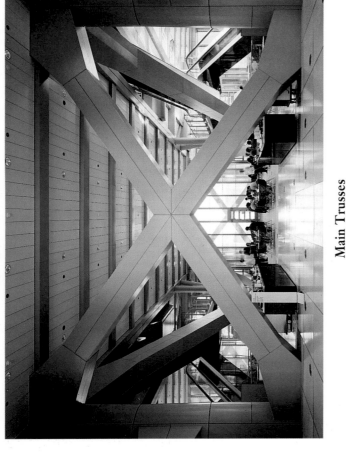

Main Trusses

Cross braces connect the main coat-hanger trusses, which are positioned at eight-story intervals. The trusses are two stories high, allowing double-height spaces within staff areas, such as elevator lobbies and the restaurant. In the elevator lobbies, passengers transfer from the elevators connecting the main lobby areas to escalators to access individual floors. This provides a greater volume of movement within the building and encourages familiarity among company employees.

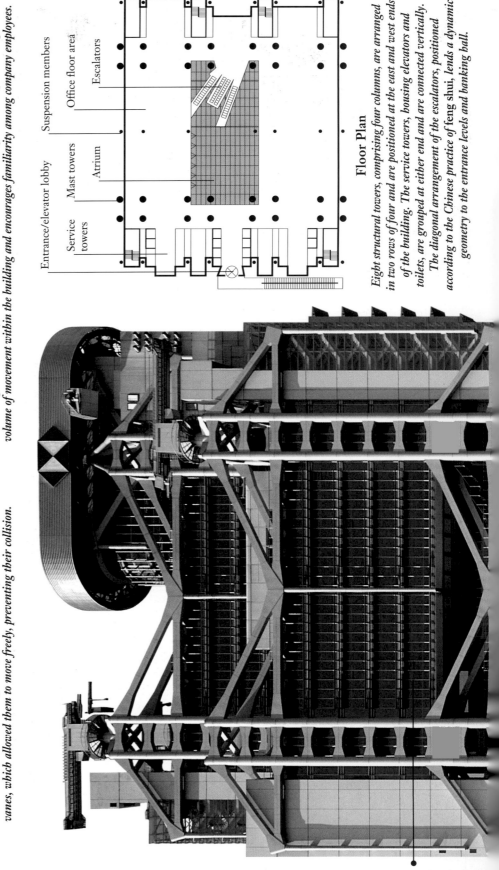

During construction, the loading cranes were mounted on the mast towers to save space on site. During high winds, when typhoon conditions made the site inoperable, the cranes were fitted with wind vanes, which allowed them to move freely, preventing their collision.

Floor Plan

Eight structural towers, comprising four columns, are arranged in two rows of four and are positioned at the east and west ends of the building. The service towers, housing elevators and toilets, are grouped at either end and are connected vertically. The diagonal arrangement of the escalators, positioned according to the Chinese practice of feng shui, lends a dynamic geometry to the entrance levels and banking hall.

Suspension members
Office floor area
Escalators
Entrance/elevator lobby
Mast towers
Atrium
Service towers

SIR NORMAN FOSTER

The architecture of Sir Norman Foster (b. 1935) embodies the integral use of technology and new materials, combined with the discipline of structural engineering.

Technology is seen as a liberating servant, allowing buildings to meet human needs in a complex and rapidly changing society. Commissions have included office buildings, airports, art galleries, and furniture design. Notable commissions are the Willis, Faber, Dumas building, Ipswich, England (1975), and the Sainsbury Arts Centre, Norwich, England (1978).

OFFICE PLANNING

Three principles were adopted in the layout of each floor: to use cellular offices to monitor points of arrival and passage; to allow the maximum number of window offices; to preserve the fluidity and transparency of space.

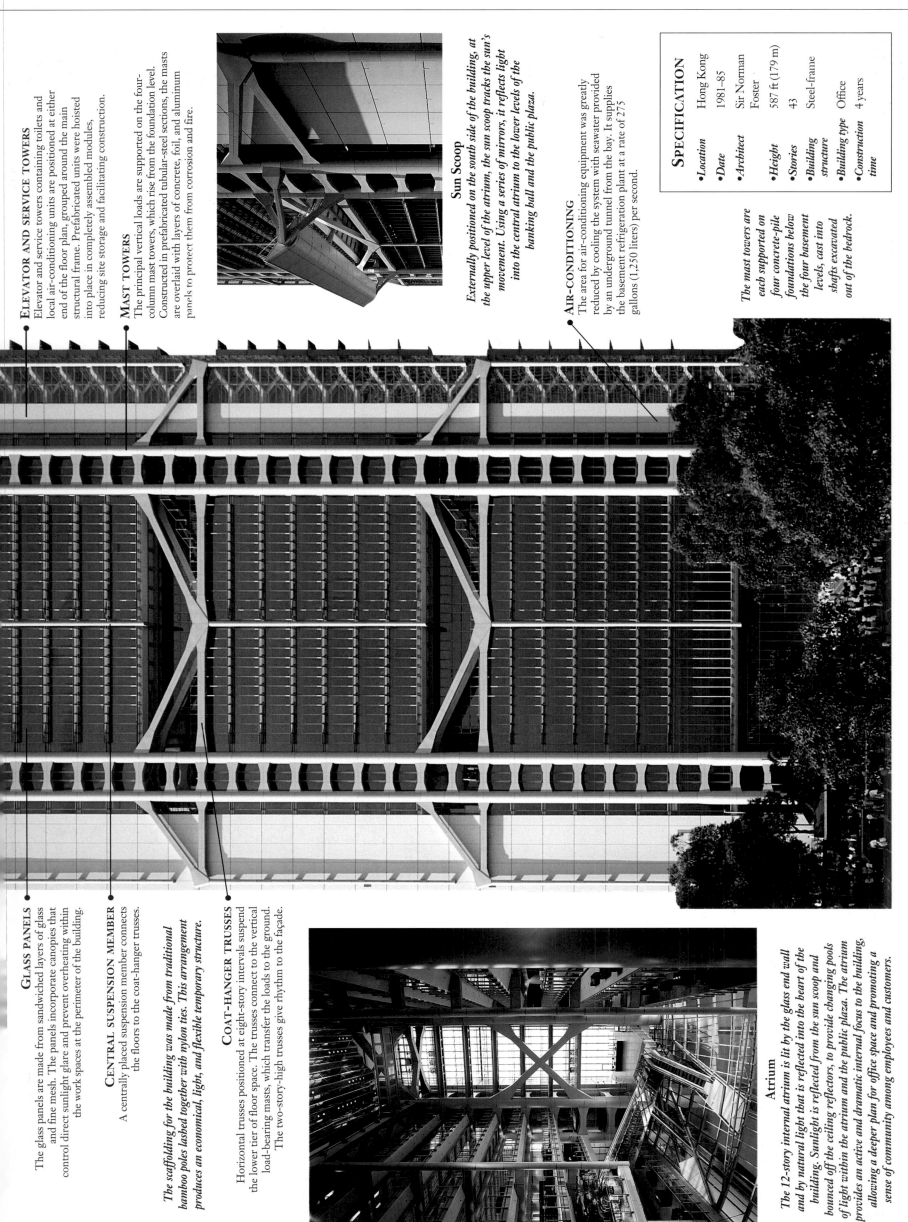

ELEVATOR AND SERVICE TOWERS
Elevator and service towers containing toilets and local air-conditioning units are positioned at either end of the floor plan, grouped around the main structural frame. Prefabricated units were hoisted into place in completely assembled modules, reducing site storage and facilitating construction.

MAST TOWERS
The principal vertical loads are supported on the four-column mast towers, which rise from the foundation level. Constructed in prefabricated tubular-steel sections, the masts are overlaid with layers of concrete, foil, and aluminum panels to protect them from corrosion and fire.

SUN SCOOP
Externally positioned on the south side of the building, at the upper level of the atrium, the sun scoop tracks the sun's movement. Using a series of mirrors, it reflects light into the central atrium to the lower levels of the banking hall and the public plaza.

AIR-CONDITIONING
The area for air-conditioning equipment was greatly reduced by cooling the system with seawater provided by an underground tunnel from the bay. It supplies the basement refrigeration plant at a rate of 275 gallons (1,250 liters) per second.

SPECIFICATION
- **Location** Hong Kong
- **Date** 1981–85
- **Architect** Sir Norman Foster
- **Height** 587 ft (179 m)
- **Stories** 43
- **Building structure** Steel-frame
- **Building type** Office
- **Construction time** 4 years

The mast towers are each supported on four concrete-pile foundations below the four basement levels, cast into shafts excavated out of the bedrock.

GLASS PANELS
The glass panels are made from sandwiched layers of glass and fine mesh. The panels incorporate canopies that control direct sunlight glare and prevent overheating within the work spaces at the perimeter of the building.

CENTRAL SUSPENSION MEMBER
A centrally placed suspension member connects the floors to the coat-hanger trusses.

COAT-HANGER TRUSSES
Horizontal trusses positioned at eight-story intervals suspend the lower tier of floor space. The trusses connect to the vertical load-bearing masts, which transfer the loads to the ground. The two-story-high trusses give rhythm to the façade.

The scaffolding for the building was made from traditional bamboo poles lashed together with nylon ties. This arrangement produces an economical, light, and flexible temporary structure.

Atrium
The 12-story internal atrium is lit by the glass end wall and by natural light that is reflected into the heart of the building. Sunlight is reflected from the sun scoop and bounced off the ceiling reflectors, to provide changing pools of light within the atrium and the public plaza. The atrium provides an active and dramatic internal focus to the building, allowing a deeper plan for office space and promoting a sense of community among employees and customers.

SCHLUMBERGER CAMBRIDGE RESEARCH CENTRE

THE SCHLUMBERGER Cambridge Research Centre (1982–85 and 1990–92) brings a distinctive silhouette to the flat Cambridgeshire landscape. Commissioned as a research-and-development facility, the architectural form, conveying the excitement of a traveling circus, harmonizes with the pastoral setting of the distant church spires. Accommodating all aspects of industrial research into oil exploration, the design integrates the conflicting spatial requirements of the large-volume industrial testing area and staff restaurant, housed under the tent enclosure, and the partitioned work spaces and laboratories, arranged in wings of single-story office suites. A second pair of buildings was added to the site in 1992, containing additional laboratories and conference rooms. The commanding spectacle of the mast-and-tent structure, particularly when internally illuminated at night, lends a theatrical image to an industrial building.

SPECIFICATION

- **Location** — Cambridge, England
- **Dates** — 1982–85 (Phase 1) 1990–92 (Phase 2)
- **Architects** — Michael Hopkins and Partners
- **Building structure** — Exoskeletal steel-frame, and tensile structure
- **Building type** — Research center

FABRIC CANOPY
The Teflon-coated canopy enclosing the testing bay is lightweight and translucent. Tension in the stretched fabric keeps the tent from flapping in the wind. The structure is designed to prevent uplift – holding the building down as well as up.

WOVEN FABRIC
The fabric, woven from glass fiber, is pattern cut from strips and seamed together by heat welding.

EXOSKELETAL FRAME
The exoskeletal (positioned outside the building envelope) frame supports the building without the additional fire-protecting layers required by internal steel structures exposed to the risk of fire.

WORK AREAS
The work spaces are housed in two single-story glass and steel-framed wings. Workstations face outward; conference rooms and laboratories face into the courtyard.

Phase Two External Wall
The first-floor glass wall is shaded by the oversailing concrete floor slab. This was constructed using a combination of precast ferro-cement coffers acting as a framework, and the in situ concrete slab. It has a highly sculptural profile, producing a lightweight section of great strength. The cost of maintaining this quality of finish is offset by savings resulting from lighter foundations, and from leaving the ceiling exposed. The coffered soffit allows for the discreet integration of lighting and an elegant, detailed junction with the column.

Phased Extension
The project was conceived as a research campus accommodating phased expansion. Phase Two included a pair of pavilions arranged along the main axis. Developments in computer-research techniques have reduced the need for reliance on the test rig, and the new blocks provide additional computer laboratories connected by a central atrium and reception area. The roof of the atrium is again a tent structure, but here is formed by a self-supporting, inflated, three-layer cushion.

Phase Two section of building

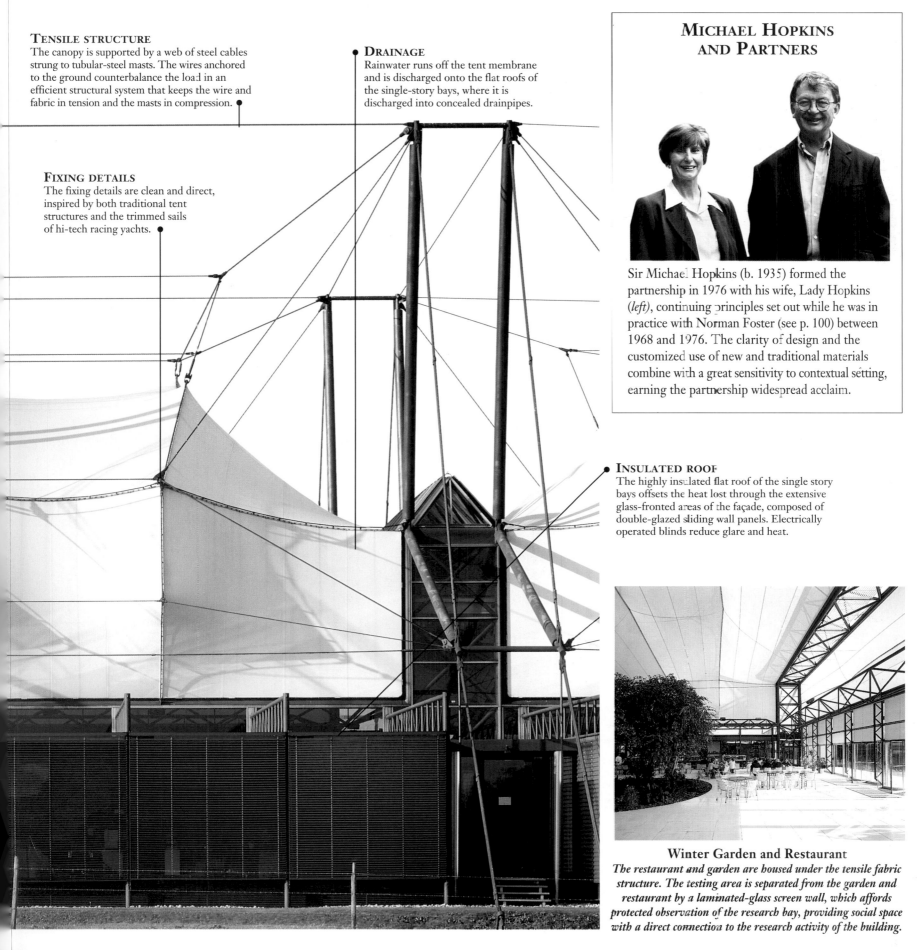

TENSILE STRUCTURE
The canopy is supported by a web of steel cables strung to tubular-steel masts. The wires anchored to the ground counterbalance the load in an efficient structural system that keeps the wire and fabric in tension and the masts in compression.

FIXING DETAILS
The fixing details are clean and direct, inspired by both traditional tent structures and the trimmed sails of hi-tech racing yachts.

DRAINAGE
Rainwater runs off the tent membrane and is discharged onto the flat roofs of the single-story bays, where it is discharged into concealed drainpipes.

MICHAEL HOPKINS AND PARTNERS

Sir Michael Hopkins (b. 1935) formed the partnership in 1976 with his wife, Lady Hopkins (*left*), continuing principles set out while he was in practice with Norman Foster (see p. 100) between 1968 and 1976. The clarity of design and the customized use of new and traditional materials combine with a great sensitivity to contextual setting, earning the partnership widespread acclaim.

INSULATED ROOF
The highly insulated flat roof of the single story bays offsets the heat lost through the extensive glass-fronted areas of the façade, composed of double-glazed sliding wall panels. Electrically operated blinds reduce glare and heat.

Winter Garden and Restaurant
The restaurant and garden are housed under the tensile fabric structure. The testing area is separated from the garden and restaurant by a laminated-glass screen wall, which affords protected observation of the research bay, providing social space with a direct connection to the research activity of the building.

Phase One section of building

THE ARK

SURROUNDED BY AN ELEVATED ROADWAY and a surface railway line, the Ark (1989–92) by Ralph Erskine establishes a strong, physical presence in a densely urban environment. The external carapace focuses the building inwardly towards the large, central atrium and protects it from noise and pollution, offering a civilizing and active social core at the centre of this speculatively built office building. The organic, pebble-shaped space increases the lettable area of the mid-level office floors while admitting sunlight on to the island site at the ground-entrance level. Erskine's experience of social housing and the inhospitable winter climate of his adopted Sweden are brought to the design of a convivial working environment. The atrium provides interlinking spaces, promoting opportunities for discussion and social interaction. The project is an imaginative, collaborative exercise between the developer and consultant designers – an attempt to introduce an enlightened view of the contemporary workplace into an unprepossessing urban site.

VIEWING TOWER
Whimsical elements break through the building envelope, such as the snorkel-like viewing tower, which provides a panoramic view from the completely glazed, informal meeting room.

ROOF LIGHT
A continuous glazed slot lights the atrium. In the event of fire, automatically opening vents and extract ducts evacuate smoke, enabling the design of the office floors to open directly on to the atrium.

VENTILATION
Computerised controls regulate the supply of air through service ducts, which prioritize natural ventilation through the atrium, reducing the need for mechanical extraction.

The appearance and form of contemporary buildings are increasingly influenced by the choice of materials and methods of environmental control, reducing energy consumption both in manufacture and running costs. About a half of all the energy produced in Western Europe is currently expended on servicing buildings.

Atrium
Naturally lit, the atrium provides fresh-air ventilation to the open office areas. The area cut out of the floor plates, producing the open atrium, provides spatial variation and direct visual contact across and between levels.

CURVED GLAZING
The curved skin inadvertently provided an externally reflective wall directing traffic noise on to surrounding streets. The building has, therefore, been criticized for detrimentally affecting adjacent sites.

TRIPLE-GLAZED PANELS
Reducing traffic to a mute spectacle, the triple-glazed panels provide an effective barrier to pollution and noise from the surrounding site.

Plan

The organically shaped plan responds both to the difficult site and to a commercial requirement to provide a high level of flexibility for a mixture of partitioned, cellular offices and open planning. The design anticipates a degree of compartmentation suitable for multitenant occupancy.

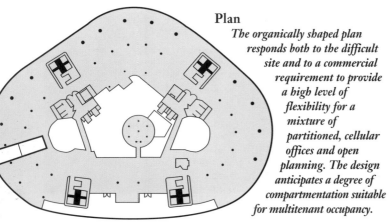

RALPH ERSKINE

Ralph Erskine (b. 1914) studied in London and has lived in Sweden since 1939. Many of Erskine's designs are generated in response to climatic conditions and social relationships. His large housing complex at Byker in Newcastle-upon-Tyne, England (1969–80), uses the form of the building to protect and nurture, providing sheltered spaces for social interaction. This principle has been adopted in a commercial context for the Ark.

● OVERSAILING EAVES
The oversailing eaves provide shelter to the terraced areas. Screened from the noise of traffic, the effects of building form, orientation, and position produce specific microclimates that can improve the immediate environment even in inhospitable conditions.

Fragmented urban sites, particularly those left around cumbersome transportation networks, provide important gaps for future city development. Although commercially undesirable, imaginative ideas are essential if pressure on the city periphery is to be relieved and urban expansion resisted, maintaining an amenable level of open space within urban streets and parks.

● COPPER ROOF
The wall panels and copper roof that conceal the ends of the floor slabs are exposed to rain and pollution and will eventually take on a weathered finish.

SPECIFICATION

●*Location*	London, England
●*Date*	1989–92
●*Architect*	Ralph Erskine
●*Building structure*	Concrete-frame and brick
●*Building type*	Offices

● LILLA HUSET
The Lilla Huset (little house), a two-story building given over to community use, was built within the site boundary. It was provided by the developer as a trade-off against commercial use of the site. This practice is known as "planning gain."

● CONCRETE STRUCTURE
The concrete frame is given additional bracing by the service towers.

Many new buildings now passively reclaim, utilize, and store the vast amounts of latent energy previously expelled during cooling and ventilation. Through a variety of active and passive methods, buildings are striving for a level of self-sustainability.

● TEXTURAL SURFACE
The bricks used for the cladding of the towers are positioned with the broken edges facing outward, providing a highly textural surface.

● ELEVATOR AND SERVICE TOWERS
The elevator and service towers rise through the building, housing stairs and elevators and a pressurized air-intake duct to supply the atrium.

KANSAI INTERNATIONAL AIRPORT TERMINAL

THE KANSAI INTERNATIONAL AIRPORT TERMINAL (1991–94) appears to hover like a glider, poised at its moment of landing, above the artificial island in Osaka Bay, Japan. Gently curving over its 1-mile (1.7-kilometer) length, the terminal joins the Great Wall of China as one of the two nonnatural structures discernible from space. Its building program required the leveling of three mountains to provide the landmass, the construction of a transportation bridge 3 miles (5 kilometers) long, and the erection of a building capable of maintaining horizontal alignment, despite anticipated site settlement of 36 feet (11 meters). The elegant design solution to the complex activities of a modern airport integrates structure, function, and environment with a sense of harmony and clarity of purpose. Its dramatic presence and inspiring sense of technological achievement make it one of the most impressive architectural projects of the 20th century.

Offshore Island
The costs and construction difficulties incurred by erecting an airport in a typhoon zone 3 miles (5 kilometers) offshore are outweighed by the advantages of a site operational on a 24-hour basis, offering future expansion and no noise restrictions.

RENZO PIANO

The work of Renzo Piano (b. 1937) has continually demonstrated conceptually and technically creative solutions to architectural, engineering, and urban-design commissions. Piano's long-time collaboration with the engineer Peter Rice has matured the raw hi-tech style of the Pompidou Center (see p. 96) through a process of continual investigation of new technologies, design methods, and computer-aided design.

SPECIFICATION

•*Location*	Osaka Bay, Japan
•*Date*	1991–94
•*Architect*	Renzo Piano
•*Building structure*	Steel-frame
•*Building type*	Airport
•*Construction time*	3 years, 2 months

COLUMNS
Each of the 900 supporting columns is continually adjusted on hydraulic, computer-controlled jacks to compensate for continual site settlement.

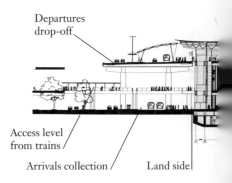

Departures drop-off

Access level from trains

Arrivals collection

Land side

LOW ROOF PROFILE
The roof profile is kept sufficiently low to allow an unobstructed view of the airplane tails from the control tower on the land side of the terminal.

ROOF FORM
The strong form of the roof produces a controlling organization for the design appreciated by arrivals by both air and train.

PLAN
The linear arrangement of the plan makes efficient use of the runway and taxiing layout, economizing on the size of the artificial island.

Toroidal Form
The toroidal form of the roof – rather like the segment of a bicycle tire – curves both across its section and along its 1-mile (1.7-kilometer) length. The 984-foot (300-meter) length of the central terminal spans 269 feet (82 meters) on tubular-steel trusses. The symmetrical wings forming the flight lounges are supported on steel ribs of different length but same curvature.

DRAINAGE
Rainwater is drained at the edge of each panel to a waterproof layer beneath. This reduces surface dirt and staining, and maintains the thermal reflectivity and appearance of the roof.

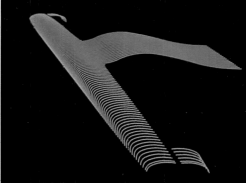

EXPANSION JOINTS
Between the structure and the skin of the building, there are expansion joints at sectional intervals that tolerate seismic and thermal movements.

CURVATURE
The gentle curvature of the roof enables all the 90,000 stainless-steel panels to be of identical size, simplifying all joints and components.

Dynamic Form
The building's form is both symmetrical and directional. The design emphasizes the movement and direction of the passengers in the same elegant and legible way that an airplane body and wing shape summarize the dynamics of flight.

TRANSPARENCY
The large areas of glass allow a transparency throughout the building, helping visitors to orient themselves and move easily to their destination within the building.

The terminal was divided between two construction teams of 4,000 to 10,000 workers – one working from the north, the other from the south, and meeting in the middle. The project was completed in three years and two months.

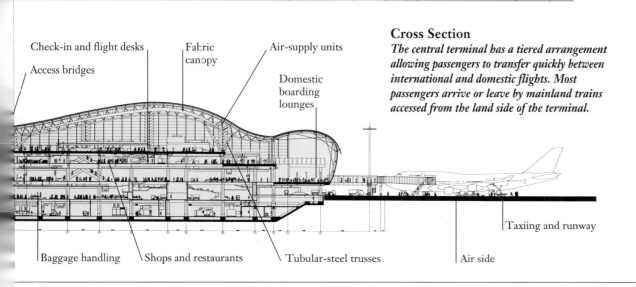

Check-in and flight desks
Access bridges
Fabric canopy
Air-supply units
Domestic boarding lounges
Baggage handling
Shops and restaurants
Tubular-steel trusses
Air side
Taxiing and runway

Cross Section
The central terminal has a tiered arrangement allowing passengers to transfer quickly between international and domestic flights. Most passengers arrive or leave by mainland trains accessed from the land side of the terminal.

Curved Roof
The length of the flight lounge wings is visually relieved by the subtly rising curve of the roof and the rhythmical articulation of the structure. The curve of the roof is aerodynamically designed to assist the movement of filtered fresh air, introduced into the terminal from large, high-level vents.

GLOSSARY

Aedicula Two columns and a pediment framing a shrine. Device used in Neoclassicism to frame a doorway or window opening.

Aisle Lower section of a church, running parallel to the nave, separated from it by columns or a screen wall.

Alberti, Leon Battista (1404–72) Architect and artist, theorist and mathematician, accomplished in many arts and sciences – exemplar of the tradition of Renaissance diversity of interests. Remembered particularly for his architectural treatise *De re aedificatoria* (1485), the first Renaissance systematic theory of proportion, order, and harmony. He defined architectural beauty as being "the harmony and concord of all the parts, achieved in such a manner that nothing could be added or taken away or altered except to the detriment to the whole."

Apse A large semicircular or rectagonal recess terminating the chancel at the eastern end of a church.

Atrium Courtyard at the center of a building that rises through consecutive floors. Derived from Roman courtyard houses, in contemporary use the atrium is often covered, providing natural light and visual contact throughout the building.

Axonometric Three-dimensional drawing projected vertically from a plan that has been rotated through an angle of 45 degrees.

Baroque A form of architecture prevalent throughout Europe during the 17th and early 18th centuries. Developed from the Classically inspired styles of the Italian Renaissance toward distinct national characteristics. Often bold, monumental, decorative, and spatially complex.

Bauhaus German school of art, craft, architecture, and industrial design, originally founded in Weimar in 1906. Led from 1916 by architect Walter Gropius (1883–1969), the school absorbed a number of European avant-garde tendencies, notably De Stijl and Russian Constructivism. The school's teachings, which joined architects, artists, and designers, became a fundamental influence in the development of modern architecture, disseminated throughout the world following its closure by the Gestapo in 1933.

Bow-string truss A composite structural device whereby the load-bearing capacity of the main beam is improved by a lower-tension chord and intermediate vertical or diagonal compression struts in the form of a horizontal bow.

Capital The crowning feature placed on the shaft of a column, primarily to spread the load transferred from the supported entablature to the column itself. Subject to stylized decoration and often used to identify the classification of architectural Order.

Centering Temporary framework, usually made of timber, used for support during the construction of arches, vaults, and domes.

Chancel Section of the east end of the nave reserved for the clergy and the choir, often separated from the nave by a screen. Also referred to as the choir.

Clerestory The upper part of a building with windows located above adjacent roofs. Found particularly in churches, allowing light to enter the nave and aisles.

Compound column Supporting column comprising multiple attached or detailed shafts. Reduces the visual mass of the support and maintains a large load-bearing cross-sectional area.

Corbel Projecting block of stone used for the support of other structural members, such as beams, or for consecutive courses of projecting stonework to produce a simple vault or dome. Often elaborately carved or molded.

Crocket Motif or leaf design carved into the projecting ribs that decorate parapets and towers of Gothic buildings and their derivatives.

Curtain wall A lightweight outside wall held off the main structural frame which serves no load-bearing purpose. A requisite of high-rise buildings and a familiar device of modern architecture, allowing a freedom of elevational composition and the use of large areas of glass in the façade.

Dentil A small, square block projecting from the cornice of a Classical entablature, providing a rhythmical façade.

Enfilade The arrangement of rooms leading from one to another. Connecting doors are often placed in alignment to produce a continuous vista when opened.

Engaged column Column with a shaft attached to or incorporated into the thickness of a wall or pier.

Entablature The upper part of an Order of architecture supported by the colonnade.

Finial Crowning ornament placed at the top of a spire or roof pinnacle.

Fluting Concave grooves carved into the shaft of a column, characteristic of Classical Orders. Produces an emphasis on vertical form and volume by creating distinctive shadow lines.

Flying buttress A buttress that stands away from the wall it reinforces, providing support via an arch at the main point of stress.

Geomancy The sacred geometry of architecture. Usually derived from alignment with auspicious groups of star constellations, the sun or moon, or axial alignment with distant or adjacent sites.

Hexastyle Classical portico with six supporting columns.

Hypostyle Hall in which the roof is supported by a multitude of columns at close intervals.

Keystone Central closing stone at the top of an arch, constructed from segmental blocks.

Kiosk A light, open pavilion or summerhouse usually supported by pillars.

Latin cross A cross with one long and three short arms. Developed from the plan of the Roman basilican church, the Latin cross accommodated lateral transepts

Detail of the entablature from
The Parthenon
See page 10

Relieving arches from
The Pantheon
See page 14

Corner Towers from
King's College Chapel
See page 40

and became the characteristic plan of the Christian church.

Lintel Horizontal supporting beam that spans an opening in a wall or between columns.

Mannerism A stylistic trend of 16th-century Italian architecture, that departed from Classical conventions of Orders and proportion to produce an exaggerated effect by subverting and manipulating architectural forms.

Metope The section of a Classical entablature between triglyphs. Left plain or with carved decoration.

Muqarnas Quintessential form of Islamic decoration and construction using an elaborately molded corbel to create the characteristic honeycomb or stalactite form of arch-and-vaulted structures.

Naos Principal chamber of a Greek temple or the core of a Byzantine church.

Nave The main body of a church to the west of the central crossing. Often flanked by aisles.

Oculus A round window.

Order Used in Classical architecture to describe the base, shaft, capital, and entablature, constituting the architectural form that conforms to prescribed proportion and decorative stylization. Principally Doric, Tuscan, Ionic, Corinthian, and Composite.

Palladianism An architectural style favored in England during the 18th century, derived from the architecture and publications of Andrea Palladio (1508–80). It spread to America in the mid-18th century and became an accepted style for grand residences and civic buildings.

Parapet A low wall screening the roof or protecting the edge of a bridge or quay.

Pavilion An ornamental building placed amid a landscaped setting. Can also be an independently expressed part of a larger building, wing, or façade.

Pediment The triangular section of wall above the entablature surmounting a portico or gable wall.

Pendentive The curved triangular surface formed between the base of the dome and the corners of the supporting structure.

Peristyle A range of columns surrounding a building or courtyard.

Piano nobile The raised floor of a building containing the principal living rooms.

Picturesque A style illustrating the late-18th-century taste for painting and architecture, depicting buildings in a landscape setting.

Pylon The gateway structure to an Egyptian temple comprising massive rectilinear towers with inclining walls.

Rationalism Architectural movement seeking to adopt rationalized and reasoned solutions to design problems, in opposition to historicist and formulaic design traditions. Usually realized through a conscious expression of structural system and constructional materials. The movement emerged through the 18th-century architecture of the French Enlightenment and was championed by French architect and critic Viollet-le-Duc, who interpreted it as an intrinsic quality of Gothic architecture. Developed throughout the 20th century in the teaching of the German Bauhaus, and by architects such as Mies van der Rohe (1886–1969), it became a central principle of Modernism.

Renaissance Derived from the Italian word for rebirth and applied to the artistic movement emanating from Italy in the 15th century. Its influence extended throughout Europe, beginning with a revival of interest in Classical architecture and developing through an extension of the Classical vocabulary into a profusion of national styles. Eventually succeeded by the Baroque period, commencing in the mid-16th century, and continuing with later developments throughout Europe.

Rib Projecting band on a ceiling or vault, often forming the primary structural frame.

Romanesque Prevalent style of architecture in western Europe from the 9th to the 12th century. Characterized by the use of the semicircular arch and simple arcaded and barrel-vaulted structures.

Serlio, Sebastiano (1475–1554) Author of *L'Architettura*, published in six parts between 1537 and 1551, giving a practical account of the Classical Orders of architecture and helping to disseminate the Renaissance throughout Europe.

Stijl (de) A small but highly influential group of architects and artists formed in Utrecht, Holland, in 1917. They sought a radical renewal of society through avant-garde methods of expression that adopted nonrepresentational form and the expansive use of planar geometry and primary colors.

Stoa Detached colonnade found in Classical Greek architecture.

Stucco Plaster work used in imitation of stone, often decoratively incised or elaborately molded.

Trabeated Structural systems comprising posts and beams used for simple support.

Transept The transverse arms joining the main nave or chancel of a church to form the characteristic cruciform plan.

Triglyph Projecting block incised with two vertical grooves, producing a rhythmic decoration on the frieze of Classical buildings.

Tympanum The expanse of wall between the lintel and the supporting arch above. Also used to describe the triangular area enclosed by the form of a pediment.

Vault An arched structure made of stone or brick covering a building. Types inlcude barrel (or tunnel), cross, fan, pendant, and rib.

Vitruvius (Active 46–30 BC) A relatively unknown Roman architect serving under Julius Caesar. Author of *De architectura*, the only surviving work on architecture passed from antiquity. Although obscurely written in ten volumes, it became a major source of reference for Renaissance architects.

Ziggurat A tower structure rising in consecutive and diminishing levels reached by stairs or a ramp.

Fine decoration from
The Taj Mahal
See page 54

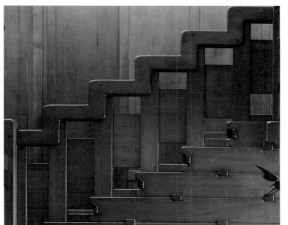

Staircase from
Gamble House
See page 76

Phase Two external wall from
Schlumberger Cambridge Research Centre
See page 102

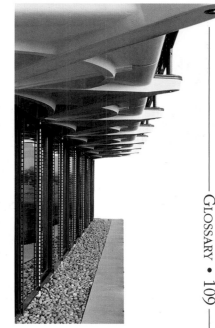

INDEX

A

Aalto, Alvar, 88
Acoustics, Sydney Opera House, 93
Acropolis, Athens, 11
Additive Architecture, 93
Adoration of the Magi, The (painting by Rubens),
40
Aedicula, 99
Aggregate, Roman, 14
Air-conditioning, Hong Kong and Shanghai
Bank, 101
  see also Ventilation
Airship mooring, 86
The Alhambra, 34–5
Altar of Heaven, 39
Altes Museum, 64–5
  inscription, 65
Amun, Temple of, Karnak, 8–9
Anchor posts, 94
Angkor Wat, 28–9
Approach: Angkor Wat, 28
  Castle Howard, 60
  Temple of Amun, 8
  Tikal, 21
Apse: Florence Cathedral, 37
  Pisa Cathedral, 25
Aqueduct, Krak des Chevaliers, 31
Arcades: blind, 47
  Pisa, 24
  St. Basil's Cathedral, 47
Arches: as structural elements, 24
  Gothic, 40, 47
  relieving, 15
  springing, 19
  structural development, 14
The Ark, 104–5
Art Deco style, 87
Arts and Crafts Movement, 67, 74, 76
Athena, statue of, 11
Atrium: The Ark, 104
  Hong Kong and Shanghai Bank, 101
Awning/Canopy: Colosseum, 13
  Neue Staatsgalerie, 99
  Potala Palace, 57
  Schlumberger Cambridge Research Centre,
  102
  Tokyo Olympic Stadium, 94

B

Balcony support, Schröder House, 83
Ball court, Tikal, 21
Baptistery, Pisa Cathedral, 24, 25
Baroque architectural devices, 60
Barry, Sir Charles, 67
Basilican form, 37
Bays, structural, 41
Blinds, solar, 96
Botanical hall, Temple of Amun, 9
Box beam, 71
Brackets: corbeled, 12
  wrought-iron, 75
Bramante, Donato, 42
  experimentation, 42, 43
Brickwork: Robie House, 79
  "Roman," 78
  Roman, 15
  Santa Sophia, 19
Brunelleschi, Filippo, 36
Burial chamber, Tikal, 20
Buttress towers, 30
Buttressing: Durham Cathedral, 26
  Notre-Dame, 32, 33
  Santa Sophia, 18
  St. Peter's, 45

C

Cables: catenary roof, 95
  supports, 94–5
Campanile, Florence Cathedral, 37
Carlisle, Lord, 60
Carrier pigeons, 31
Castle Drogo, 80–1
  stepped levels, 81
Castle Howard, 60–1
Cathedral builders (medieval), 33
Causeway, Angkor Wat, 28
Ceiling bosses, 40
Central crossing: Pisa Cathedral, 25
  St. Paul's Cathedral, 59
Chandella kings, 23
Chapel of the Nine Altars, Durham, 27
Chatsworth House, 69
Choir, Durham Cathedral, 27
Choir screen, King's College Chapel, 41
Chrysler Building, 7, 86, 87
Citadel, fortified, 34
Cladding: Empire State Building, 87

Gamble House, 76
granite, 93
Menier factory, 70
Sydney Opera House, 93
timber, 88
Villa Mairea, 88
woven fabric, 102
Classical devices, 49
Clock Tower, Houses of Parliament, 67
Cloister of San Pietro, 42
Coat of arms, King's College Chapel, 41
Coffering: Altes Museum, 65
  Florence Cathedral, 36
  Pantheon, 15
Colonnades: Altes Museum, 64
  Angkor Wat, 28
  Pisa Cathedral, 24
  St. Peter's, 45
The Colosseum, 12–13
Color schemes: primary colors, 83
  white, 85, 89, 90
Columns: as structural elements, 24
  compound, 27
  Corinthian, 14, 44
  Doric, 10
  hydraulically adjusted, 106
  Ionic, 64
  Ise Shrine, 16
  Kansai Airport, 106
  multiple shafts, 40
  paired freestanding, 59
  Pantheon, 14
  Parthenon, 10, 11
  piloti, 84
  Pompidou Center, 97
  rusticated, 47
  Sagrada Familia, 73
  Temple of Amun, 8, 9
  three-quarter, 12
  Tuscan, 43
  Villa Mairea, 88
  water-filled, 97
Concrete: The Ark, 105
  exposed, 95
  oversailing floor slab, 102
  Roman, 13, 14, 15
  structural frame, 105
  substructure, 96
  supporting mast, 94
Construction: Angkor Wat, 28
  brick skin, 19
  Colosseum, 12, 13
  Empire State Building, 86
  enveloping structure, 63
  exoskeletal frame, 102
  exposed framework, 71
  factors affecting modern, 104
  Farnsworth House, 91
  Hong Kong and Shanghai Bank, 100
  iron framework, 63, 66, 69, 71
  Kandariya Mahadev Temple, 23
  Kansai Airport, 107
  Pantheon, 14
  Pompidou Center, 96, 97
  Schröder House, 83
  shoin style, 53, 76
  steel framework, 86, 90, 96, 97
  Temple of Amun, 9
  Tikal, 21
  timber-framed, 52–3, 76–7
  traditional Japanese, 77
  Villa Mairea, 89
  see also Domes/Dome construction
Construction materials: ashlar stone, 21, 60
  Colosseum, 13
  granite, 81, 93
  Khmer, 29
  Pantheon, 14
  reuse of Roman, 25, 43
  sandstone, 23
  see also Brickwork; Concrete; Stonework
Cornices, Egyptian, 98
Corridors, Castle Howard, 60
Cosmology, Roman, 14
Court of the Lions, Alhambra, 35
Courtyard palace, 34
Courtyards: Alhambra, 34
  Neue Staatsgalerie, 99
  Potala Palace, 57
Craftsman, The (magazine), 76
Crockets, 40
Cross: St. Peter's, 44
Crypt: St. Peter's, 45
  Tempietto San Pietro, 43
Crystal Palace, 68–9
Cupolas, restraining, 15
Curtain wall, Menier factory, 70

D

Dado, marble, 54
Dalai Lama, 57
  tombs of, 56
De re aedificatoria (book by Alberti), 48
De Stijl group, 82

Decoration *see* Ornamentation
Defense lines, Krak des Chevaliers, 30
Dialogue Concerning Two New Sciences (book by
  Galileo), 58
Dom-ino Skeleton, 84
Domes/Dome construction: Castle Howard, 60
  coffered, 15, 65
  Florence Cathedral, 36, 37
  Pisa Cathedral, 25
  pointed/melon-shaped, 36
  Royal Pavilion, 63
  Santa Sophia, 18, 19
  spherical volume, 14
  St. Basil's Cathedral, 46
  St. Paul's Cathedral, 58
  St. Peter's, 45
  Taj Mahal, 55
  Tempietto San Pietro, 42, 43
Doorway of Charity, Sagrada Familia, 73
Doorway of Faith, Sagrada Familia, 73
Durham Cathedral, 26–7

E

Eaves, overhanging/oversailing, 52, 74, 76
Elevation: Castle Drogo, 81
  Castle Howard, 61
  St. Paul's Cathedral, 58
  St. Peter's, 44, 45
Elizabeth I, Queen, 50
Embankment, Houses of Parliament, 67
Empire State Building, 86–7
Energy conservation, 104–5
Entablature, Parthenon, 10, 11
Entasis, 10, 11
Entrance: Krak des Chevaliers, 31
  Neue Staatsgalerie, 99
  Temple of Heaven, 38
Erskine, Ralph, 105
Escalator, Pompidou Center 97

F

Façades: Castle Drogo, 81
  Durham Cathedral, 27
  Glasgow School of Art, 74, 75
  Hardwick Hall, 51
  Houses of Parliament, 67
  Notre-Dame, 32
  St. Paul's Cathedral, 59
  St. Peter's, 44
  stucco, 62
  Villa Savoye, 85
Farnsworth, Edith, 90
Farnsworth House, 90–1
Fencing, Ise Shrine, 17
Feng shui, 38
Ferdinand and Isabella of Spain, 34, 43
Finials: *chigi*, 17
  "pompom," 72
Fire-proofing/Fire-escape, Pompidou Center,
  97
Fittings, decorative, Ise Shrine, 16
Five Points for a New Architecture (book by Le
  Corbusier), 84
Floors: Houses of Parliament, 66
  Menier factory, 71
  Pompidou Center, 97
  removable, 13
Florence Cathedral, 36–7
Flying buttresses, 33
Formwork, 14
Foster, Sir Norman, 100
Friezes: Hardwick Hall, 50
  Parthenon, 11
  Tempietto San Pietro, 43
  Temple of Heaven, 39

G

Gable wall, 24
Galilee Chapel, Durham Cathedral, 26
Galleries: Altes Museum, 64
  Angkor Wat, 29
  Santa Sophia, 18
Gamble House, 76–7
Gardens: Alhambra, 35
  Hardwick Hall, 51
  Katsura Palace, 52, 53
  planting boxes, 78
  roof garden, 84–5
Schlumberger Cambridge Research Centre,
  103
  Taj Mahal, 54–5
  Villa Mairea, 88–9
  Villa Savoye, 85
  see also Landscape
Gas lighting, 62
Gaudí, Antonio, 72
  wire models, 72
Generlife, Alhambra, 34
Geometry: elemental forms, 49
  planar, 82
Gerberettes, 96
Giotto, 37

Glacis, Krak des Chevaliers, 31
Glazing: Crystal Palace, 68–9
  curved, 104
  Glasgow School of Art, 75
  Gothic, 32
  Hong Kong and Shanghai Bank, 101
  Sydney Opera House, 92
  triple-glazed panels, 104
Gothic architecture: Florence Cathedral, 36–7
  King's College Chapel, 40–1
  Notre-Dame, 32–3
  Victorian revival, 66–7
Greek Revival, 64
Greene, Charles Sumner, 76
Greene, Henry, 76
Gropius, Walter, 52

H

Hadrian, Emperor, 15
Hall: Castle Howard, 61
  Gamble House, 77
  Hardwick Hall, 50
  Temple of Heaven, 39
Hall of Kings, Alhambra, 35
Handrails/Railings: Glasgow School of Art, 75
  Neue Staatsgalerie, 99
Hardwick Hall, 50–1
Harmon, A. L., 86
Hatshepsut, Obelisk of, 9
Hawksmoor, Nicholas, 61
"Heart pillar," 16
Henry VI, King, 41
High Great Chamber, Hardwick Hall, 50
Hong Kong and Shanghai Bank, 100–1
Hopkins, Michael, and Partners, 103
Houses of Parliament, 66–7
Hunchback of Notre-Dame, The (book by Hugo),
  32
Hypostyle hall, Temple of Amun, 8, 9

I

Imperial apartments, Potala Palace, 56
Inauguration games, Colosseum, 13
Industrial architecture, 70–1
Ise Shrine, 16–17
Islamic architecture, 34–5
  principles, 54, 55
Island, artificial, 106
Ivan IV (the Terrible), 46

J

Jali screen, 62
Jones, Inigo, 60
Julius II, Pope, 42
Justinian I, Emperor, 18

K

Kandariya Mahadev Temple, Khajuraho, 22–3
Kansai International Airport Terminal, 106–7
Katsura Palace, 52–3
  architects inspired by, 52
King's College Chapel, 40–1
Kiosk of Taharka, Temple of Amun, 8
Knights Hospitaller, 31
Krak des Chevaliers, 30–1
Kremlin, Moscow, 47

L

Lamb, T., 86
Landscape: "Arcadian," 48
  Castle Howard, 61
  Farnsworth House, 90
  Gamble House, 77
Lantern: Florence Cathedral, 36
  Schröder House, 83
  St. Paul's Cathedral, 58
  St. Peter's, 44
Laws of Motion (book by Newton), 58
Le Corbusier, 52, 85
  Purist experimentation, 84
Library, Glasgow School of Art, 75
Lilla Huset, 105
Loggia, vaulted, 30
Lutyens, Sir Edwin, 81

M

Machiocoulis, 30
Mackintosh, Charles Rennie, 75
Mahal, Mumtaz, 55
Mannerism, 98
Mantegna, 42
Marble, use of: Durham Cathedral, 27
  Farnsworth House, 90, 91
  Florence Cathedral, 37
  Parthenon, 10
  Pisa Cathedral, 24, 25
  Taj Mahal, 54
  Temple of Heaven, 39
Mask, Temple of the, 21
Mast towers: Empire State Building, 86

Hong Kong and Shanghai Bank, 101
Masts, Tokyo Olympic Stadium, 94
Metabolist group, 95
Michelangelo, 45
Mies van der Rohe, Ludwig, 90, 91
Minarets, 18, 54, 55
Minimalism, 91
Modern Movement, 84, 85
Modernism, 65, 68, 70, 99
Mogul Indian architecture, 62–3
Mondrian, Piet, 82
Music Room, Brighton Pavilion, 63

N

Namgyal Monastery, 56
Nash, John, 62
Nasrid rulers, 35
Nativity scene, Sagrada Familia, 73
Nave: Pisa Cathedral, 25
  Sagrada Familia, 73
  Santa Sophia, 19
Neoclassicism, 65, 98
Neue Staatsgalerie, 98–9
Niches: Glasgow School of Art, 74
  King's College Chapel, 41
  Pantheon, 15
  Tempietto San Pietro, 42
Notre-Dame, Paris, 32–3
Notre-Dame-du-Haut, Ronchamp, 85

O

Obelisk: St. Peter's, 44
Office planning, Hong Kong and Shanghai
  Bank, 100
Old Palace of Westminster, 66
Olympic Stadium, Tokyo, 94–5
Onion-shaped domes, 46, 63
Open planning, Robie House, 79
Opera House, Sydney, 92–3
Orientation: St. Peter's, 44
  Temple of Heaven, 38
Ornamentation: Alhambra, 35
  calligraphy, 54
  Crystal Palace, 69
  gilding, 57
  Houses of Parliament, 66, 67
  Islamic, 54
  King's College Chapel towers, 40
  Menier factory, 70
  muqarnas, 35
  murals, 65
  Notre-Dame, 33
  Pantheon floor, 15
  Potala Palace, 57
  Robie House, 79
  St. Paul's Cathedral, 59
  symbolic, 73
  Tempietto San Pietro, 43
  Temple of Amun, 8
  textural bricks, 105

P

Palace of Industry for All Nations, 69
Palladian style, 61
Palladio, Andrea, 49
  architectural theory, 48
The Pantheon, 14–15
Paradise gardens, 35, 54–5
The Parthenon, 10–11
Partitions, non-load-bearing, Farnsworth
  House, 90
Patio de la Acequia, Alhambra, 34
Paul III, Pope, 45
Pavement, Temple of Heaven, 39
Pavilion of Laughing Thoughts, Katsura, 53
Paxton, Joseph, 69
Paxton gutter, 68
Pediment, St. Paul's Cathedral, 59
Pentelic marble, 10
Pericles, 10
Peristyle: The Parthenon, 10
  Tempietto San Pietro, 42
Perpendicular style, 40–1
Piano, Renzo, 97, 106
Piano nobile: Villa Rotonda, 48
  Villa Savoye, 84
Piazza of St. Pietro, Rome, 44
Piers: brick, 79
  Colosseum, 12
  compound, 32
  Notre-Dame, 32
  Robie House, 79
  Santa Sophia, 19
Pieta (sculpture by Michelangelo), 45
Pinnacles, 40
Pisa Cathedral, 24–5
Pisano, Andrea, 37
Plans: Altes Museum, 64
  The Ark, 105
  Farnsworth House, 90
  Hong Kong and Shanghai Bank, 100
  Kandariya Mahadev Temple, 23

Kansai Airport, 107
Neue Staatsgalerie, 98
Robie House, 78
St. Basil's Cathedral, 46
Taj Mahal, 55
Tempietto San Pietro, 42
Villa Rotonda, 49
Villa Savoye, 84
Platforms/Plinths: Gamble House, 76, 77
  Ise Shrine, 17
  Kandariya Mahadev Temple, 22
  Potala Palace, 57
  St. Basil's Cathedral, 47
  Taj Mahal, 54
  Temple of Heaven, 39
  Villa Rotonda, 49
Podium: Neue Staatsgalerie, 99
  St. Basil's Cathedral, 47
  Sydney Opera House, 93
Pompidou Center, 96–7
Porch: Pantheon, 14
  Robie House, 79
  Schröder House, 82
  Villa Mairea, 89
Portal, Notre-Dame, 32
Portico: Kandariya Mahadev Temple, 23
  Pantheon, 14
  St. Peter's, 45
  Villa Rotonda, 49
Potala Palace, 56–7
Prayer towers *see* Minarets
Prefabrication, 96
Prince Regent, 62
Processional route: Potala Palace, 57
  Sydney Opera House, 92
Pugin, A. W. N., 67
Pylons, Temple of Amun, 8

Q

Quattro libri (book by Palladio), 48

R

Rainwater runoff: Crystal Palace, 68
  Kansai Airport, 107
  Katsura Palace, 52
  Schlumberger Cambridge Research Centre,
    103
Ramses II, 9
Raphael, 44
Rationalism, 70
Reception area, Villa Savoye, 84
Red–Blue Chair, Schröder House, 82
Reform Club, London, 67
Renaissance architecture, 47
Repton, Humphry, 62
Restaurant, Schlumberger Cambridge Research
  Centre, 103
Ribs: Durham Cathedral, 26
  Florence Cathedral, 36
Ridge billets, 17
Rietveld, Gerrit, 83
Robie House, 78–9
Rogers, Richard, 97
Romanesque architecture: Florence Cathedral,
    36–7
  Pisa Cathedral, 24–5
Roof vents, 66
Roofs: cantilevered, 78
  copper, 105
  crenellated ridge, 20
  curved, 107
  insulated, 103
  Katsura Palace, 52
  marquee form, 63
  Pantheon, 15
  suspended structure, 94–5
  Temple of Heaven, 38
  Tokyo Olympic Stadium, 94–5
  toroidal, 107
Rose window, Durham Cathedral, 27
Royal apartments, Alhambra, 35
Royal Pavilion, 62–3
Royal Throne, Houses of Parliament, 67

S

Sacred Mountain, Kandariya Mahadev Temple,
    22
Sagrada Familia, 72–3
Sampietrini, 45
Sanctuary: Kandariya Mahadev Temple, 23
  Temple of Amun, 9
  Tikal, 20
  see also Shrines
Sanctuary (protection), 26
Santa Maria del Fiore *see* Florence Cathedral
Santa Sophia, 18–19
Saulnier, Jules, 70
Scandinavian design, 89
Schinkel, Karl Friedrich, 65
Schlumberger Cambridge Research Centre,
    102–3
School of Art, Glasgow, 74–5

Schröder House, 82–3
  isometric projection, 83
Schröder-Schrader, Truus, 82
Screens *see* Walls
Scrollwork, 51
Sculpture/Statuary: Alhambra, 35
  Altes Museum, 64
  Angkor Wat, 29
  Castle Howard, 61
  Kandariya Mahadev Temple, 22, 23
  Notre-Dame, 32
  Parthenon, 11
  Sagrada Familia, 73
  scrollwork, 51
  St. Paul's Cathedral, 58, 59
  Tikal, 20
Sculpture terrace, Neue Staatsgalerie, 98
Seating levels, Colosseum, 12
Services: Castle Drogo, 81
  Castle Howard, 60
  Pompidou Center, 96
  Sydney Opera House, 93
  Villa Savoye, 84
Shah Jahan, 55
Shinto (religion), 17
Shoden, Ise Shrine, 16, 17
Shoin, 52, 53, 76
Shokintei, 52
Shreve, R. H., 86
Shrewsbury, Countess of, 50
Shrines: Ise, 16
  Potala Palace, 57
Sikhara, Kandariya Mahadev Temple, 22
Skylights, 95
Skyscrapers, 87
Sleeping platforms, 76
Smythson, Robert, 50
Spectators, Colosseum, 13
Sphinxes, Avenue of, Temple of Amun, 8
Spire, Notre-Dame, 33
St. Basil's Cathedral, 46–7
St. Cuthbert, 27
St. Paul's Cathedral, 58–9
St. Peter's, Rome, 44–5
Staircase: Farnsworth House, 91
  Gamble House, 77
  Hardwick Hall, 51
  Royal Pavilion, 62
Stelae, Tikal, 21
Steps: Altes Museum, 65
  Pantheon, 14
  Parthenon, 11
Stirling, Sir James, 99
Stoa, 64
Stonework: Angkor Wat, 28, 29
  Castle Howard, 60
  Glasgow School of Art, 75
  Neue Staatsgalerie, 98
Sun scoop, Hong Kong and Shanghai Bank, 101
Symbolism, structural: St. Basil's Cathedral, 46
  Temple of Heaven, 39

T

Taj Mahal, 54–5
Talenti, Francesco, 37
Tallest building, 87
Talman, William, 61
Tange, Kenzo, 94, 95
Tatami, 52
Taut, Bruno, 52
Tea ceremony, 53
Tempietto San Pietro, 42–3
Temple I, Tikal, 20–1
  ritual activities, 20
Temple Mountain, Angkor Wat, 29
Temple of Heaven, 38–9
Temple of the Four Winds, Castle Howard, 61
Temple of the Great Jaguar, 20–1
Tent-and-tower churches, 46
Terraces: The Ark, 105
  Neue Staatsgalerie, 98
  Tikal, 20
  Villa Mairea, 89
  Villa Savoye, 84
Tiers: Colosseum, 12
  Temple of Heaven, 39
Tiles: ceramic, 38, 93
  redwood shakes, 76
Towers: Angkor Wat, 28, 29
  The Ark, 104
  campanile, 72
  Durham Cathedral, 27
  elevator and service, 101, 105
  Hardwick Hall, 51
  Houses of Parliament, 66, 67
  Kandariya Mahadev Temple, 22
  King's College Chapel, 40
  Krak des Chevaliers, 30, 31
  Notre-Dame, 32
  Santa Sophia, 18, 19
  St. Paul's Cathedral, 58
  Taj Mahal, 54
  Temple of Amun, 8
  see also Mast towers

Tracery: Indian derived, 62
  Islamic, 35
Transepts: Kandariya Mahadev Temple, 22
  Notre-Dame, 33
  Pisa Cathedral, 25
Trusses, 96
  coat-hanger, 100, 101
Turbine Building, Menier factory, 70–1
Turret staircase, 62
Turrets, Temple of Heaven, 39
Tympanum wall, Santa Sophia, 19

U

Utzon, Jørn, 92, 93

V

Vanbrugh, Sir John, 61
Vases: Altes Museum, 64
  Robie House, 79
Vaults/Vaulting: Angkor Wat, 29
  brick, 71
  fan, 92
  Gothic, 41
  pointed-rib, 26
  ribbed, 26
  Romanesque, 24
  Taj Mahal, 55
  see also Ribs
Ventilation: computerized control, 104
  Crystal Palace, 68
  Houses of Parliament, 66
  Katsura Palace, 53
  Potala Palace, 56
Veranda, Katsura Palace, 53
Vespasian, Emperor, 13
Victoria, Queen, 62
Victoria Tower, Houses of Parliament, 66
Viewing tower, The Ark, 104
Villa Mairea, 88–9
Villa Rotonda, 48–9
  miniaturized derivation, 61
Villa Savoye, 84–5
Villa Surbana, 49
Viollet-le-Duc, Eugène 33, 70
Vishnu (Hindu deity), 28

W

Walking City (project by Ron Herron), 97
Walls: Castle Drogo, 80–1
  glass, 96
  Ise Shrine, 17
  Krak des Chevaliers, 30
  Pisa Cathedral, 24
  Potala Palace, 56, 57
  screen, 34, 41, 63
  sloping, 80
Wastell, John 40
Water, use of: Alhambra gardens, 35
  Katsura lake, 53
  Khmer projects, 28, 29
  Krak des Chevaliers, 31
  sacred lake, 9
  Taj Mahal, 54–5
Wheel of Life, Potala Palace, 56
Windmill, Krak des Chevaliers, 31
Windows: arched Romanesque, 98
  bay, 74, 78, 89
  Castle Drogo, 80
  clerestory, 19, 33, 58
  corner, 83
  Durham Cathedral, 27
  Empire State Building, 87
  false, 51
  full-length plate-glass, 91
  Glasgow School of Art, 74, 75
  Hardwick Hall, 50, 51
  inset, 75
  King's College Chapel, 41
  Menier factory, 71
  mullioned, 80
  ocular, 15, 49
  ribbon, 85
  slotted openings, 30
  Temple of Amun, 9
  traceried, 40
  see also Glazing; Skylights
Workforce: cathedral builders, 33
  Ise Shrine, 16
  Santa Sophia, 18
  Taj Mahal, 54
Wren, Sir Christopher, 59, 60
Wright, Frank Lloyd, 52, 76, 79
Wyatt, James, 62

Y

Yunglo (third Ming emperor), 38
Yusuf I, 35

Z

Zoning Laws (New York), 86

ACKNOWLEDGMENTS

Author's acknowledgments

I should like to acknowledge Neil Lockley, Simon Murrell, Julie Oughton, Deborah Pownall, Gwen Edmonds, and Christine Winters for their dedication throughout the project; and to thank Sean Moore for his encouragement. In addition,

I would like to thank all at Sagar Stevenson Architects for their patience during my periodic absence while undertaking this work. My thanks also to Melanie and Louis for their constancy and companionship.

Dorling Kindersley would like to thank:

Will Hodgkinson, Karen Homer, Rebecca Munford for editorial assistance; Kathy Gill for the index; Robert Polidori for additional photography, and Deborah Pownall for her splendid picture research.

PICTURE CREDITS

Every effort has been made to trace the copyright holders and we apologize in advance for any unintentional omissions. We would be pleased to insert the appropriate acknowledgment in any subsequent edition of this publication.

Key
t: top, *b*: bottom, *c*: centre, *r*: right, *l*: left

Aerofilms 60*tr*.
AKG/ Eric Lessing 64-5, 65*tl*.
Annan Gallery, Glasgow 75*bc*.
Arcaid back cover trc, back cover br, back cover bc, 4*tl*, 4*c*, 10*cl*, 37*bl*, 46-7, 48*tr*, /Richard Bryant 50-1, 51*tr*, /William Tingey 53*tr*, /Clay Perry 60-1, 66*tr*, 72*bl*, 74*tl*, 75*bc*, 75*br*, 78-9, 79*tl*, 79*tr*, /Richard Bryant 80-1, 80*cl*, 84-5, 86-7, /William Tingey 94*tl*, 95*cr*, /Richard Bryant 98-9, 98*bl*, 100*tl*, 101*bl*, 102-3*b*, 104-5, 104*bl*, 106-7, 108*bl*.
Archigram Archives/ Ron Herron 96*tr*.
Axiom/ Jim Holmes 14*tr*, 16*cl*, 17*tr*, 17*cr*, 29*tl*, 34-5, 45*tr*, 52*cl*.
Bridgeman Art Library 9*tl*, 13*tc*, 13*cr*, 27*tl*, 31*tr*, 33*tl*, 46*tr*, 55*tc*, 59*br*, 68*tr*, 69*t*.

The British Architectural Library, RIBA, London 69*cr*.
British Museum 11*tl*.
Camera Press 72*bl*, 91*tl*, 96*br* both, 105*tr*.
Centraal Museum, Utrecht/Rietveld Schröder Archives back cover tl, 82-3, /© Beeldrecht 82*bl*, 82*tr*, 83*tl*, 83*tr*.
Corbis 79*cr*, 86*tr*, 86*br*.
Joe Cornish back cover tr, 48-9.
James Davis Travel Photography 13*tl*, 15*br*, 28-9, 39*tr*, 44*cl*, 72-3.
Design Press /Lars Hallen 88-9, 88*tr*, 89*tl*, 89*tr*.
Esto Photographics 76-7, 77*tl*, 77*tr*, /Scott Francis 90-1, 90*bl*, 91*tr*, 109*bc*.
e.t. archive 10*tr*, 18*bl*, 53*tc*.
Mary Evans 11*cr*, 15*tr*, 41*cr*, 45*cr*, 58*tr*, 61*tl*, 62*tr*, 67*cl*, 69*br*.
Eye Ubiquitous 73*cl*.
GA Photographers 94-5.
Dennis Gilbert 3, 102-3*tc*, 102*bl*, 103*cr*, 109*br*
Glasgow School of Art 74*tr*, /Ralph Burnett 74-5.
Greene and Greene Library, Pasedena 76*tc*, 76*tr*.
Sonia Halliday 18*tr*.
Robert Harding Picture Library front cover *tl*, font cover *tr*, back cover cl, 4*tl*, 4*bl*, 4*br*, 7*bl*, 8*tl*, 9*tr*, 19*tr*, 21*tr*, 23*tr*,

25*tl*, 26*tr*, 28*tl*, 29*tr*, 30*tl*, 31*tl*, 32-3, 32*tr*, 32*cl*, 33*tl*, 36*cr*, 39*br*, 40*tl*, 40*tr*, 45*tl*, 46*tl*, 54*cl*, 54*tr*, 56-7, 57*tr*, 71*tl*, 85*cr*, 88*bl*, 93*cr*, 96*tc*, 108*br*, 109*bl*.
Michael Hopkins and Partners /Richard Davies 103*tr*.
Angelo Hornak 2, 6*c*, 12*cl*, 26-7, 27*bc*, 42-3, 42*tr*, 58*tl*, 66-7, 67*tc*.
Hulton Getty 11*tr*, 49*tl*, 67*tl*, 68-9, 81*br*, 93*tr*.
Kansai International Airport Co Ltd 7*tr*, 106*tl*, 107*t*, 107*br*.
A. F. Kersting front cover cl, front cover c, back cover bl, inside flap t, 5*bl*, 6*tl*, 10-11, 30-1, 30*bl*, 36-7, 40-41, 41*bl*, 54-5, 58-9, 59*bl*, 61*tr*, 62-3, 96*tl*.
Ian Lambot back cover cr, 1, 5*tr*, 100-1, 100*tr*, 101*tr*.
Le Corbusier Foundation © ADAGP, Paris DACS, London 1997 84*tr*, plans 84*cl*, 84*bl* Le Corbusier re-drawn by Janos Marffy.
Link 17*tl*.
Mansell Collection 42*br*.
Simon Murrell 23*tl*, 46*br*, 90*cl*, 100*cr*, 105*tl*.
Museum of Scotland, Edinburgh 20*bl*.
National Palace Museum, Taiwan 38*bl*.
National Trust Photographic Library 50*cl*, 50*tr*, 51*tl*, 81*tl*, 81*tr*.

Moh Nishikawa front cover cr, 16-17, 52-3.
Renzo Piano Building Workshop, Geneva/Stefano Goldbert 106 *bl*, 107*b*, 107*cr*.
Resource Photo/Pankaj Shah 22*tr*, 22*bl*, 23*cr*.
Royal Pavillion Art Gallery and Museums, Brighton 63*tl*, 63*tr*.
Kenzo Tange Associates 95*tl*, 95*tr*.
Trip Photographic Library 21*cr*, 22-3.
Temple Expiatore of the Sagrada Familia, Barcelona 72*tr*.
Scala 42*bl*.
South American Pictures 20-1.
Roger-Viollet 85*tc*.
Michael Wilford and Partners Ltd 98*tr*, 99*tr*.
Frank Lloyd Wright Archives 78*tr*, Frank Lloyd Wright Drawings are copyright © 1997 The Frank Lloyd Wright Foundation.
Zefa back cover ct, back cover cl, 5*br*, 8-9, 8*bl*, 12-13, 18-19, 24-5, 36*tr*, 38-9, 39*cr*, 44-5, 56, 57*tl*, 67*tr*, 92-3, 92*tr*, 93*tl*, 99*tl*.